The Earth

The Earth

CONTENTS

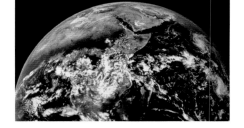

PLANET EARTH

The Earth is 4.6 billion years old. Together with seven other planets, it orbits the sun, and is in turn orbited by the moon. One hemisphere is always closer to the sun than the other because the Earth's axis is slightly tilted – that's why there is summer and winter. Because the Earth spins around its axis, we have day and night. Despite the regularity of these physical facts, the Earth has not always developed in a constant way. Traces left in the Earth's rocks tell of past natural catastrophes. Time and again, creatures have became extinct, and new ones have emerged. This process is still continuing even today.

What is the Milky Way?

If you look up into the sky at night you discover that the stars are not evenly spread. A bright band trails its way across the sky – the Milky Way. It contains the stars of our galaxy. Our sun is one of countless stars in a spiral of stars and dust turning around a central point. Hardly anything is so far known about the centre of the Galaxy. It lies behind a thick veil of dust.

What is a solar system?

A solar system is a sun with all the planets and smaller bodies that move around it as the central point. Perhaps every star we see is the centre of a solar system.

How far away are the planets from the sun?

At an average distance of 58 million kilometres (36 million miles), Mercury is the closest planet to the sun. The average distance from the sun of Neptune, the most distant planet, is 4,500 million kilometres (2,800 million miles).

How many stars are in our galaxy?

Our galaxy contains around two billion stars. One of them is our sun. It whizzes around the centre of the Galaxy at the enormous speed of 900,000 kilometres (more than 550,000 miles) per hour.

The Earth is the only inhabited planet in our solar system.

Starting with the Sun in the centre, the planets orbit the sun in the following order: Mercury, Venus, the Earth, Mars, Jupiter, Saturn, Uranus and finally Neptune. Mercury, the Earth, Venus and Mars have solid surfaces. Jupiter, Saturn, Uranus and Neptune, on the other hand, are gigantic balls of gas.

In what order do the planets orbit the sun?

This is how the Earth may have formed.

There are many likely theories. The first is the Nebular Hypothesis, according to which a spinning cloud contracted and became the sun. Rings then split off and condensed to become planets and moons. The second is the Tidal Theory: a passing star tore material from the sun, which then became the planets. The third, the Supernova Theory, suggests that the Sun had an accompanying star that exploded. Its debris became the planets. According to the Dust Cloud Theory, particles of dust clustered together to form clumps. Many swarms of these clumps then became the planets.

How was the Earth created?

Johannes Kepler was a German astronomer who lived from 1571 to 1630. He was the first person to set out a precise model of the Solar System. Kepler discovered that the planets orbit the sun on elliptical paths.

Who was Johannes Kepler?

Other inhabited planets cannot be ruled out, but there are none in our solar system. The nearest star to our sun that may also have planets is 40 trillion kilometres (25 trillion miles) away. That is so far away that it would take the fastest spaceship 60,000 years to reach it. Even if there is life somewhere else in the Universe, it is unlikely that we will ever meet aliens.

Do aliens exist?

How are the seasons created?

The Earth takes almost exactly a year to orbit the sun, and its axis is slightly slanted at an angle. That is why one hemisphere is always tilted more towards the sun than the other. The side facing the sun gets more sunshine every day, and in summer the sun doesn't even set at all at the poles. The side of the Earth leaning toward the sun also receives more warmth than the one experiencing winter.

Why do people born on 29th February stay young?

The time it takes the Earth to completely orbit the sun once is called a solar year. It is exactly 365.26 days long and therefore about six and a quarter hours longer than a calendar year. An extra day is added to the calendar every four years to compensate for this difference. These years with 366 days are called leap years. There's a 29th February only every four years. Sometimes, because the difference between a solar year and a calendar year is slightly more than six hours, a leap year has to be skipped. Then people born on 29th February have to wait eight years to celebrate their birthday!

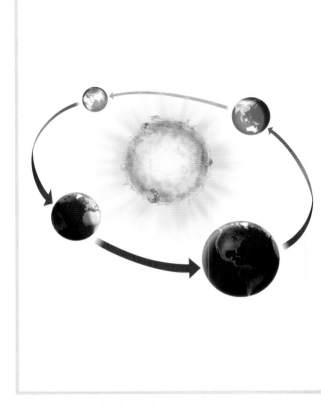

It takes one year for the earth to orbit the sun.

Why is it light during the day?

The Earth turns around its axis once every 24 hours. When the place where we live is on the side of the Earth facing the sun, it is daytime and the sun shines. The sun is at its highest at midday, when we are closest to it. At sunset, the sun's rays reach us only at a sloping angle, and not at all at night.

What are shooting stars?

Sometimes shooting stars can be seen on a clear night. As opposed to real stars, they shoot across the sky at great speed and burn up. Most shooting stars can be seen in August. They are meteoroids, small pieces of stone the size of a pebble, which come from space, enter the Earth's atmosphere and burn up due to friction with the air.

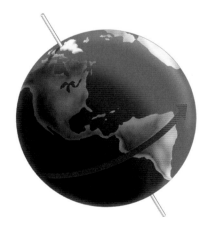

The Earth's axis is tilted at an angle. It is summer on the side turned to the sun.

Today's most important instruments for observing the sun are Ulysses and SOHO, two probes orbiting the sun. People have to be very careful when looking at the sun directly because the light is so strong it damages the eyes. A sun filter, for example glasses coated with a dark film, must always be used. The sun can also be observed using ocular projection – the projection of an optical picture of the sun from a telescope onto a screen. During a solar eclipse, the moon almost covers the sun. Only a bright ring can be seen – the corona.

During a solar eclipse, the moon covers the sun. Only a thin bright ring can be seen: the Corona.

What does the surface of the sun look like?

The sun is covered with bubbles that are about twice as big as Great Britain. They bubble away like water boiling in a pan. But instead of water, the sun consists of hot plasma, a mixture of gases.

When does the sun disappear during the day?

Sometimes, from our perspective, the moon stands directly in front of the sun. Then we have a solar eclipse on Earth. Of course, the moon is much smaller than the sun. But because it is much nearer the Earth, its circumference is enough to completely cover the sun. At first, a crescent of the sun like a crescent moon can still be seen. This becomes smaller and smaller. Then the sun disappears completely. Only a few rays around the moon can still be seen. A total eclipse lasts only a few minutes. Then the moon moves slowly on and lets the sunlight fall on the Earth again.

What is a planet?

A planet is a celestial body that orbits a star. The Earth is a planet. It orbits a medium-sized star, the sun.

What is so special about Stonehenge?

Stonehenge is a construction in southern England that was built between 3,100 and 2,000 BC. The position of the circle of large vertical standing stones is aligned to the solstice and equal length of day and night. It is for this reason that it is thought to have served as an observatory, although research on this point has not yet been completed.

What are sunspots?

Sunspots are dark patches on the visible surface of the sun. They are cooler than the rest of the surface and therefore radiate less light.

Do other planets also have moons?

A moon is a celestial object that orbits a planet. It is kept in orbit by the planet's gravity. All planets in our solar system have moons except for Mercury and Venus. Saturn has at least 22!

Why is there no Man in the Moon?

With a little fantasy, a man can be seen in the moon when a full-moon is looked at closely. But in reality, these are meteorite craters. Very many boulders of rock from space hit the moon because it has no protective atmosphere. The lack of an atmosphere is also the reason why there is no life on the moon, neither a man, nor fish, nor lichen.

When did the first human set foot on the moon?

On 20th July 1969 the American Neil Armstrong became the first human to step onto the moon. The Apollo project was abandoned in 1972 because of the high costs.

Who owns the moon?

An international agreement that came into force in 1984 prohibits countries or individuals from claiming ownership rights over the moon. The moon therefore belongs to no one.

The largest of the moon's craters can be seen from Earth.

In spite of all the legends, there is no life on the moon.

Meteorites hit the Earth less often than the moon because most extraterrestrial boulders of rock burn up in the atmosphere. But a boulder from space did, for example, cause the indentation of the Nördlinger Ries and the Steinheimer Basin in southern Germany. The Earth has not been hit by any meteorites worth mentioning for a long time. The largest to be found during the last hundred years was discovered in Namibia in 1920. It weighed only 60 tons.

Are there meteorite craters on Earth?

After it was formed, the moon came close to the Earth. Because it was smaller and therefore had less gravity it was pulled by the Earth, began to turn more slowly, and the Earth's gravity caused the side facing the Earth to bulge.

Why does the moon have a bulge?

The Earth does not have a bulge. No heavier celestial object has affected it. But it is nevertheless not completely round. It is flattened at the poles. This is caused by the centrifugal force that is created when an object spins. Centrifugal forces can also be felt when a skipping rope is spun around.

Has the Earth also got a bulge?

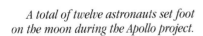

A total of twelve astronauts set foot on the moon during the Apollo project.

Is the Earth hollow like a football?

No. The Earth has a hard outer layer, the Earth's crust. Underneath this is not air but, instead, the Earth's mantle consisting of both liquid and solid rock. The Earth is built up from a total of five layers: the Earth's crust, the upper and lower mantle, and the outer and inner core. This core mostly consists of iron.

Why do I land back on the Earth when I jump up?

The Earth's large mass attracts the comparatively small mass of a person. This process is called gravity or gravitation. The Earth's gravity not only prevents you from disappearing off into space when you jump, it also guarantees that the air we breathe stay around the Earth as its atmosphere. This is also why a rocket needs very strong propulsion to leave the Earth's atmosphere.

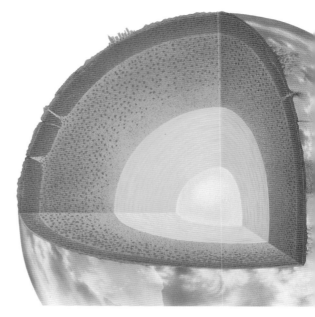

The Earth is built up from a total of five layers: the inner and outer core, the lower and upper mantle, as well as the Earth's hard, but very thin, crust.

What is geochemistry?

Geochemistry is the science dealing with the chemical composition of the Earth. It has discovered that the most common elements are iron, oxygen, magnesium and silicon. In this, great differences exist between the Earth's crust, mantle and core.

The Earth's gravity is very strong. Rockets and space shuttles need a great deal of propulsion to overcome it.

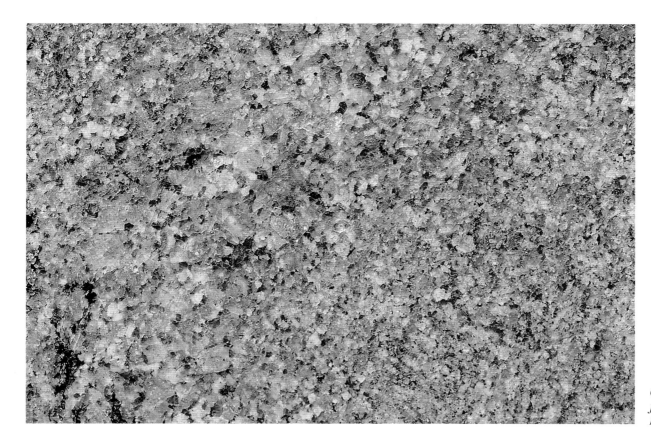

Granite is cooled magma from underneath the Earth's surface.

Does rock melt in the Earth's mantle?

It is so hot under the Earth's crust that stone turns to liquid. This liquid stone is called magma. The Earth's crust is made up of cooled magma that has become solid again.

What can studying earthquakes tell us about the structure of the Earth?

When the Earth shakes, the tremors create shock waves. These waves can be measured by a device called a seismograph. The waves travel along the surface at a different speed than into the Earth. This can help us to reach conclusions about the composition of the Earth.

Scientists have often bored holes in the Earth. But they have never gone very deep compared to the Earth's diameter. When a nine-kilometre-deep hole (more than 5 ½ miles) was bored in Windisch-Eschenbach in Bavaria, the temperature was found to be 270 degrees Celsius at this depth. That is hotter than the temperature needed to bake a cake. The temperature increases one degree every 30 metres. A twelve-kilometre-deep hole has been bored on the Kola Peninsula, in Russia, which is almost half the thickness of the Earth's crust. Compared with the Earth's diameter, that is like sticking a drawing pin into a football.

The Earth's inner core is between 5,100 and 6,370 kilometres (3,100 and 3,900 mile) from the Earth's surface. It would be necessary to bore down 2,900 kilometres (1,800 miles) to reach the outer core. This is roughly the distance from Lisbon to Stockholm.

How do we know it's hot inside the Earth?

How far away is the Earth's core?

Why is it so difficult to show the Earth on a map?

The Earth is round. The best way to show it is on a globe: on a map in the shape of a ball. But maps are often flat. It is not easy to show something round on a flat surface. This can easily be seen with a broken inflatable ball. It is difficult to press it flat even when it is cut up. Many so-called projections are used when making maps. That's what the techniques for showing the world as a map are called. But none of them is really a true reproduction of the surface and scale.

What is the ideal scale for a hiking map?

On a map of the world with a scale of 1:100,000,000 for instance, one centimetre on the map represents one hundred million centimetres or 1,000 kilometres in nature. The continents can easily be recognised on such a map. But a map with a scale of 1:50,000 should be used for hiking, while a scale of 1:100,000 is sufficient for cycling.

What does an umbrella on a map mean?

An umbrella on a map does not mean that the area in question gets a lot of rain. Small umbrellas usually mark bathing areas or beaches.

Maps display the curved surface of the Earth on a level surface.

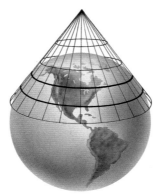
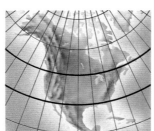
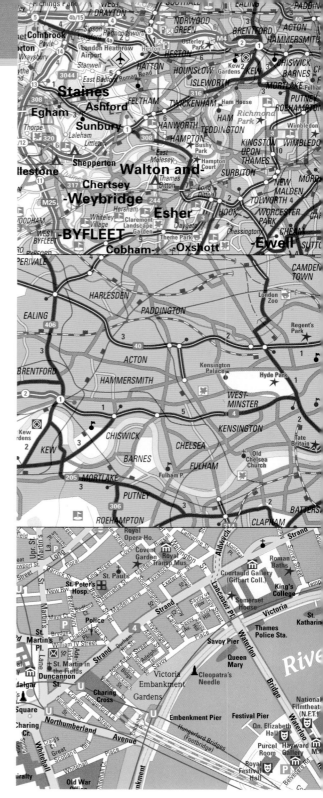

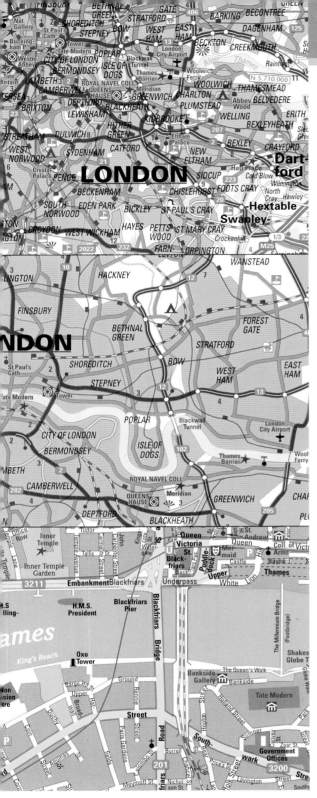

A map of the city of London in three different scales: 1:301,000, 1:150,000 and 1:12,500. The larger the scale, the more precisely the landscape, roads and even individual houses can be recognised. A distance of eight centimetres on the bottom map is equivalent to one kilometre in reality.

Should legends be trusted?

That depends. On the one hand, the word "legend" is the name used for stories about saints and heroes which are in part true and in part made up. But legend is also the word used for the box on a map that explains it. The legend explains how a train station is depicted or how a capital city is marked.

How can the length of a route be measured with a piece of string?

By laying a piece of string on a map it is possible to measure the route to school. When the map is to the scale of 1:100,000 and the length of the route on the map measured by the piece of string is eight centimetres, then the real route is 8 times 100,000 centimetres, or eight kilometres.

What are contour lines?

Contour lines indicate how steep a mountain is. If it slopes gently upward, the lines are far apart. When they are very close together, the rock face is almost vertical. All points along a contour line are the same height above sea level.

How are maps made?

Maps were made earlier using rough measurements made on the spot. Today, cartographers mainly use aerial photographs or photographs shot from space.

This satellite photograph of the Himalayas with Mount Everest at the top left serves cartographers as a guideline when making a map.

How can the Earth's history be read from rocks?

So-called sedimentary rocks have formed in layers during the history of the Earth. They consist of deposits of sediment. When a volcano has erupted anywhere in the world, it has, for example, left a layer of ash that can be seen today in stone.

What is stratigraphy?

Reading layers of rock is called stratigraphy. Geologists identify the individual layers according to the size of the grain, the minerals they contain and the colour. They compare layers of rock from various places on Earth and can then say something about their history. A greater time span in the Earth's history can be seen from the edge of the Grand Canyon than from anywhere else on Earth. The rocks here are between 750 and 225 million years old.

What is a geologic time scale?

After stratigraphically studying them, geologists can draw up a chart showing the order of the Earth crust's various layers of rock. This sequence is known as the geologic time scale. The various levels are named according to periods of time, of which there are basically three: the Archean, the Proterozoic and the Phenerozoic, which extends up to the present day.

Brown coal is created when peat sinks down: brown coal mining near Cologne.

The history of the Earth can be read from the layers of rock lying on top of one another. Peat lies at the very top, while anthracite lies in the lower layers.

The various layers of rock can often be seen where roads or railways have been built into steep slopes.

The sedimentary layers of the Earth's crust have been formed in quite different ways. Limestone was created when the shells of animals and plants, mostly in the sea, were deposited. Gypsum and rock salt were formed where seas evaporated. Peat and coal developed from piled-up plants that grew on land a long time ago.

What has turned to stone over time?

Petrology is a science that belongs to geology. It is the study of rocks, their composition and the conditions in which they were formed and changed.

What is petrology?

In most places where we live the Earth's crust is covered by trees and fields. But the sequence of layers can still be seen clearly where a steep slope provides no hold for soil, or where a river cuts deep into the ground. Man inflicts many wounds on nature. When roads or railways cut a straight path through hilly ground, the layers of rock can be seen along the edges.

How does road building help geologists?

Often fossils of fern seeds can be found when rocks from the Antarctic are examined. The Antarctic was not yet at the South Pole during the Permian period, about 250 million years ago. The climate was then so warm that plants could grow.

Was the Antarctic always so cold?

Sandstone formed in Europe during the Permian period, the Earth's most recent period about 290 to 250 million years ago. At that time Europe was subject to a hot desert climate. This is shown by the strongly rounded individual grains. They were transported by the wind.

When did Europe have a desert climate?

How can the age of fossils be determined?

Fossils, petrified plants and animals, are seldom found alone. They are usually found with other fossils in a layer. Some of them are found all over the world. Creatures have developed further over time. Tiny, single-cell organisms became multi-cell plants and animals. It is known that life developed in the same order on all the continents and that every species of animal developed only once in the course of history, and has never re-emerged after once becoming extinct. So when layers of rock are found with similar fossils, it is assumed that they were formed about the same time.

How did plants and animals turn to stone?

Most dead animals or plants rot away quickly. Their bones or wood remain a little longer. Some skeletons were covered by the seabed or the bed of a lake. They stopped rotting. Mineral solutions embedded themselves in them, making the fossils harder and turning the bones or wood into stone.

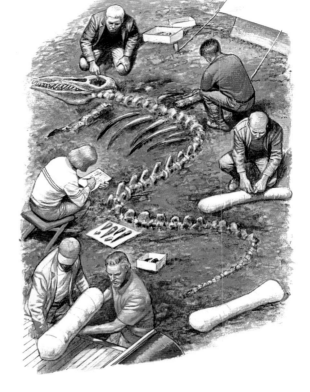

Palaeontologists examining the petrified remains of a sea reptile.

What is palaeontology?

Palaeontology is a science that concerns the development and conditions of life during the history of the Earth. Fossils form an important part of palaeontological research.

What fossils can be found in the permafrost?

Fossils can also be formed by freezing. In Siberia and Alaska, in cold regions where the ground remains frozen throughout the year, complete mammoths and woolly rhinoceroses have been found.

The skull of a Tyrannosaurus: fossils show what dinosaurs looked like.

What are fossil fuels?

Crude oil, natural gas and coal are known as fossil fuels because they are the remains of prehistoric life forms.

The age of rocks can be determined on the basis of index fossils. When the same fossil is found in the rocks in different locations it can be concluded that these rocks are of roughly the same age. Index fossils have to fulfil certain conditions, however: the species of animal or plant must have existed for only a short time. They must have been widespread geographically, and the fossils must be identifiable beyond doubt.

Sometimes, fossils are not dead petrified animals or plants but their impressions, which have been filled by mineral solutions. Fossils of burrows, animal tracks or excrement have formed this way. Amazing footprints of dinosaurs can be seen today in Sataplia Nature Park in Georgia.

Are fossils necessarily be the remains of dead animals or plants?

Land animals did not yet exist at that time. Instead, countless numbers of creatures lived in the sea. There were jellyfish, sponges, annelids and starfish, among others.

Where did many animals live 500 million years ago?

Natural gas is a fossil fuel.

The remains of trilobites are among the most important fossils. Together with many other groups of animals, these creatures appeared more than 545 million years ago during the so-called Cambrian explosion, the starting shot for the development of animals. Characteristic of them is a large head and a flat shell. They moved by crawling or swimming and fed on worms and small creatures. Some of them grew to almost two metres in length. They had large shell shields on their heads and tails. Their body shields, the shell around the stomach, could be moved to let them roll up into a big ball – just like woodlice, their present-day relatives.

What are trilobites?

The Tyrannosaurus had teeth up to 18 centimetres (7 inches) long. But the teeth were of different lengths depending on how old they were. If a Tyrannosaurus lost a tooth, another one would grow in its place. The teeth did not change once during a lifetime, but continually when needed. A tooth would be lost every now and then because the Tyrannosaurus caught its prey with its jaws and feet. But with 50 teeth, there were always enough tools left to do the work.

How long were the teeth of a Tyrannosaurus?

What is a cephalopod?

Cephalopod is a specialist name for water creatures that sit in a snail-like shell. Only the creature's head sticks out. Ammonites were cephalopods with rolled, flat, grooved shells. On the basis of their fossils, it is possible to date the 370 to 365 million-year-old layers of rock.

What was the Cretaceous period?

There were still no people in the Cretaceous period, between 145 and 65 million years ago. But the white chalk of today was formed during the Cretaceous period. It consists of the shells of billions of tiny sea organisms. This layer is often so thick that chalk cliffs have formed, such as those in Rügen, Germany.

What were the first mammals?

The first mammals developed about 220 million years ago. They were small and looked like rats. They were probably only active at night.

Who was Lucy?

The skeleton of a human who lived about three million years ago was found in Ethiopia in 1974. This person was named Lucy. She could walk upright on two legs, but was only just over a metre tall.

Not many groups of animals from the age of the dinosaurs have survived. Crocodiles and caimans are still around today.

The chalk cliffs on Rügen were formed from the shells of tiny micro-organisms.

All animal species, including horses, have changed and developed further over time.

Palaeontologists knew about coelacanths from fossils. They have a three-lobed tail. Their fins are set out like arms. They appeared during the Devonian age, about 400 million years ago. Scientists believed for a long time that these animals had died out. But in 1938 a fisherman caught a living coelacanth off the coast of South Africa. This species is therefore a so-called living fossil. Further examples were later found and filmed.

Are there living fossils?

The largest flying creatures were the flying reptiles of the age of the dinosaurs. The Pteranodon is surely the best known of them. Its wings had a span of eight metres (over 25 feet). It mainly fed on fish. The Pteranodon disappeared at the end of the Tertiary period, as did all other dinosaurs. Tortoises and crocodiles survived.

What were the largest flying creatures?

The oldest horse found, the Hyracotherium, was as big as a dog. Older horse remains have four toes, more recent ones three. Modern horses have a hoof. Over the course of development, the teeth became larger and firmer, and horses were able to chew increasingly harder types of grass.

Have horses always looked like they do today?

EARTH'S STRUCTURE

The Earth is continually changing. We people hardly notice many of these changes because they occur very slowly. Some parts of the Earth move further apart due to the continental plates shifting, others move closer. High, snow-capped mountains or very deep sea trenches can be formed in the process. On the other hand, wind and ice also erode the stone, whereby the mountains shrink again. Some volcanic eruptions and earthquakes happen so suddenly that people and animals in the regions affected are taken by surprise and enormous damage is done.

Would it have been possible to walk to Australia 250 million years ago?

Yes, because Australia as we know it today did not yet exist then. Columbus would not have needed a ship to discover America 75 million years ago. It lay very close to the British Isles. And he could have made a quick trip to the Antarctic to rest under palm trees from his strenuous journey. 250 million years ago Australia, America and the Antarctic belonged to Gondwana, the prehistoric supercontinent. It later broke apart and the individual pieces drifted across the globe.

Are the continents still shifting?

The continents do not move great distances in a short time, but Europe and America are still drifting apart. The distance between Munich and New York increases by 22 millimetres (almost an inch) every year, and Santiago de Chile even moves 75 millimetres (almost three inches) away. But then Hong Kong drifts almost a centimetre (just under half an inch) closer to us every year.

Today, most species of marsupials live in Australia. The Koala is also a marsupial.

When did people discover that the Earth changes?

Quite exact maps of the Earth began to be made as early as in the 16th century. People were surprised that the coastlines on both sides of the Atlantic fitted into one another like the pieces of a jigsaw puzzle. People began to ask themselves even then whether the continents had at some-time been close together.

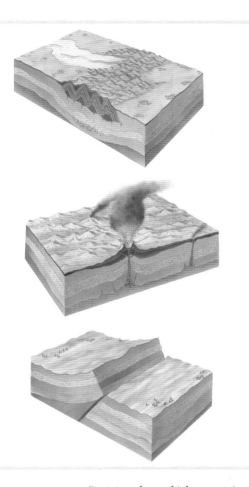

Deep trenches or high mountains are formed where plates meet.

The German geophysicist Alfred Wegener, who lived from 1880 to 1930, proved the theory of continental drift. Apart from coastlines that fitted together, he also pointed out similar layers of rock and identical fossils on various parts of the Earth as proof.

Who was Alfred Wegener?

Glowing, liquid magma can be found under the Earth's hard crust. The land masses slide about over this slippery layer. The Earth's crust and the Earth mantle consist of individual plates called lithospheric plates. They are shifted by movements inside the Earth. Where two plates meet, they slide under one another. One plate is pushed down into the depths and the other folds to form mountains. The Earth's crust tears where plates are pulled apart. Magma swells up, creating mountains on the seabed.

Why don't the continents stay where they are?

Two to three million years ago there were armadillos only in South America. They were initially trapped in their native habitat because they couldn't swim. A land bridge to North America was created when Panama rose from the sea. The Armadillo then spread northward.

How did the armadillo get to North America?

Marsupials developed about 200 million years ago on the prehistoric supercontinent of Gondwana. The present-day Antarctic drifted slowly southward. The climate grew steadily colder, until the marsupials finally froze to death.

Why are there no marsupials still living in the Antarctic?

Some plates slide past each other in opposite directions. The Pacific plate and the North American plate rub together at the San Andreas Fault. Strong earthquakes occur when they get caught.

What is the San Andreas Fault?

Why are sea fossils found in the Alps?

The Alps were formed by two lithospheric plates colliding. An ocean was formed between Africa and Europe when the prehistoric supercontinent broke apart. It was situated where the Alps are found today. Sea creatures such as ammonites lived in it. Their shells pilled up on the seabed. Then, 100 million years ago, the African continent pushed northward and the sea disappeared. The land mass folded and the Alps were created. The fossils of the sea creatures were pushed upward and now lie at a height of several thousand metres.

The ice of a glacier, such as this one in South American Patagonia, drags rubble along with it.

Why is the seabed off South America melting?

An oceanic and a continental plate meet on the western side of South America. The seabed of the Pacific Ocean slides under the South American plate, where it melts because the interior of the Earth is so hot. Liquid magma is formed. This rises under the west coast of South America and reaches the surface when volcanoes erupt.

How are glaciers created?

Glaciers are created when large amounts of snow on mountain ranges do not melt. The snow is compressed to form rivers of ice that wander downhill. The ice also drags rubble with it, which is then deposited as a moraine.

Skiers and snowboarders often unintentionally cause avalanches in deep snow.

Mountains and mountain ranges have been created in various places on Earth by continental drift.

What are avalanches?

When it thaws in the mountains or snow is shaken, newly fallen snow begins to slide. An avalanche pulls more and more snow with it on its way downhill and can also bury people under it.

When are deserts created in the lee of mountains?

Mountains form a wind barrier. It rains particularly heavily on the side from which the wind comes. On the other side of the mountain the wind has lost its moisture. That's why deserts like the Mojave Desert in North America form behind mountains.

The deepest sea trench is the Mariana Trench. Here one oceanic lithospheric plate slides under another. The upper plate, the Philippine plate, is younger, thinner and not as heavy; the other, the Pacific plate, is descending. A trench has formed where these two plates meet. It is 10,924 metres (35,800 feet) deep and could swallow the world's highest mountain, Mount Everest.

Edelweiss first spread to the Alps during the last Ice Age. It can also be found in the Pyrenees, the Carpathian Mountains and in the Balkans. Edelweiss originally flowered in the Siberian Steppes. Although it doesn't need rocks to grow well, it has a better chance of surviving in inaccessible places. Edelweiss is on the red list of plants threatened with extinction. On no account should it be picked.

Could Mount Everest disappear into a trench?

Has edelweiss always blossomed in the Alps?

How can we see that mountains age?

People are annoyed when they wrinkle with age. Things are different with mountains. They become lower and smoother. High mountains are younger than low ones. All mountains are subject to the ravages of time: wind and rain wear them away.

Why doesn't the rock ptarmigan sink in the snow?

Animals that live in snow-covered mountains have to make sure that they don't sink in the snow. The rock ptarmigan has feather collars growing around its feet. Its body weight is then spread over a larger surface and pressure is reduced.

What are fjords?

A fjord is a steep and narrow arm of the sea that stretches far inland. The valleys were once dug by rivers or glaciers and later filled by water as the sea level rose.

Why is the highest mountain on Hawaii?

With its 8,848 metres (29,000 feet), Mount Everest is considered the world's highest mountain although Mauna Kea on Hawaii. measures 10,205 metres (33,500 feet). However, only 4,200 metres (13,780 feet) rise above the surface of the sea.

The Alps are a relatively young mountain range. The famous Matterhorn in Switzerland can be seen here.

The air contains less oxygen the higher one climbs. More air must be breathed in to supply the body with the oxygen it needs. That's why people from low-lying areas who go hiking in the Alps gasp for air. In the case of people and animals in Peru and Chile, their bodies have already adapted to the altitude. The inhabitants of the Himalayas also have bigger lungs.

Why do people and animals in the Andes have bigger lungs?

You notice for yourself that a warm pullover is needed on the peak of a mountain. The air becomes progressively thinner with increasing altitude and can store less warmth. The temperature sinks on average 6.5 °C every 1,000 metres (3,330 feet). So if the temperature at 500 metres is 16 °C, it is only 0 °C at 3,000 metres. That's why snow doesn't melt even in summer in high mountain areas.

Why is there snow on high mountains?

Chamois and ibex live from roaming. In summer they jump over the rocks in high lying areas and look for food on mountain meadows. However, in winter it is also too cold for these animals. They move lower down into the valley and look for shelter from the icy wind in the woods.

For whom is mountaineering vitally important?

Snow lies on high Alpine peaks even in summer, as seen here with the Gorner Glacier.

In summer the ibex look for food on meadows high in the mountains, but in winter they descend into the valleys.

What is a volcano?

A volcano is an opening where liquid, solid or gaseous material is discharged from inside the Earth. Volcanoes can spew out boulders of rock, lava, water steam or sulphur gases.

Are all volcanoes dangerous?

Gentle volcanoes are not dangerous. Thin-flowing lava bubbles up evenly out of the ground and people and animals can easily seek shelter. Such volcanoes can be found on Hawaii. By contrast, the eruption of highly explosive volcanoes is unpredictable. Their magma is thick. It cools and becomes solid before it reaches the surface. It then blocks the volcano's outlet. The magma below tries to push up and suddenly the pressure blows the plug into the air. The stone can be blown up to 80 kilometres (50 miles) into the sky. People living close to the volcano are in great danger.

What types of volcanoes are there?

Volcanoes come in different shapes and sizes depending on how they are formed geologically. Shield volcanoes have a wide, flat cone. They are created when thin-flowing lava spreads far before it becomes hard. Stratovolcanoes on the other hand are steeper. They are made up of many layers of lava, a new one being added with every new eruption.

A volcano is an opening in the Earth's crust where molten rock is discharged from inside the Earth.

Basalt is cooled lava: here a waterfall over basalt cliffs.

A geyser spraying water in Iceland.

The Volcano of Etna, on the island of Sicily, Italy, stands 3,332 meters high. It came into being about 600,000 years ago and still erupts fairly often even today.

Which is the highest volcano in Europe?

Bread-crust bombs are not weapons of war made by a baker. They are boulders of lava slung out of a volcano. They often rotate while in the air and become round. From a distance they look like loaves of peasants' bread when their surface tears in flight.

What are bread-crust bombs?

Basalt is cooled lava. When the lava layer that pours from a volcano is thick, it cools very slowly. Cracks appear during cooling. These split the basalt into hexagonal columns.

What is a basalt column?

Almost the whole of Europe lay under a thin layer of dust following the eruption of the Laki volcano on Iceland in 1783.

Why was Europe so dusty in 1783?

Geysers are hot springs with water fountains. A hot fountain of water shoots up at almost regular intervals. Underground, hot volcanic rock brings water to a boil. This leads to hot springs. In some places the underground water is heated up so much that it turns to steam. The steam rises and pushes up the cooler water above it as a fountain. There are geysers on Iceland, New Zealand and in Mexico. The most famous geyser is "Old faithful" in the USA. It erupts regularly every 73 minutes. The water then shoots 40 metres (130 feet) high for two to five minutes.

What is a geyser?

What causes earthquakes?

Earthquakes can accompany volcanic eruptions or be caused by hollow spaces underground collapsing. Most earthquakes are so-called tectonic quakes. There are places where the Earth quakes especially often, for example in Japan or in California in the USA. These areas lie on the edges of lithospheric plates. These move over the Earth's mantle at a roughly constant speed. But the rock of the Earth's crust cannot move as easily. Suddenly the tension is too great and the Earth's crust jerks. Earthquakes are therefore actually an everyday event.

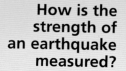

Do earthquakes happen in Germany?

The ground can shake in Germany too, but no earthquake has destroyed houses or killed people in the last 500 years. Occasionally there are slight shakes in the Hohenzollern Trench in southwest Germany, but normally nothing more than the clinking of glasses is heard.

Two thirds of Lisbon was destroyed by an earthquake in the 18th century.

How is the strength of an earthquake measured?

Scientists compare the strength of earthquakes on the Richter Scale. People cannot feel an earthquake under magnitude two. It can only be recorded by a sensitive measuring instrument, the seismograph. The crockery in the cupboard begins to rattle at magnitude four. Cracks appear in walls and tiles are shaken from the roof at magnitude six. Earthquakes of magnitude eight have terrible consequences if they occur in inhabited areas. Earthquakes often also cause fires because gas pipes burst and the gas ignites.

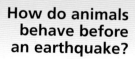

How do animals behave before an earthquake?

Animals seem to be better at noticing the dull underground rumble that precedes an earthquake. Horses try to break out, mice and snakes leave their holes.

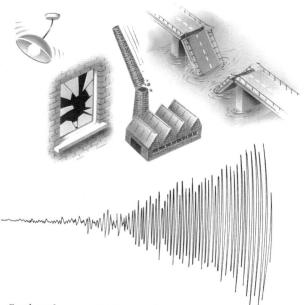

Earthquakes can slightly rock the ground or cause devastating damage, depending on their strength.

The Richter Scale measures the strength of an earthquake on an open scale. Every step upward means a tenfold increase in energy. The strongest earthquake measured so far reached a strength of 9.2. By contrast, the twelve stages of the Mercalli Scale measure an earthquake according to the damage it causes. At stage one, water vibrates in a glass. Stage twelve means heavy damage to the landscape and buildings.

What should I do when the earth shakes?

On no account run outside when the earth begins to shake. Between houses is the likeliest place to be hit by falling roof tiles. If already outside, you should run to an open space with no buildings or trees nearby. If an earthquake suddenly happens when indoors, the best thing to do is to go to the smallest room of the house, the toilet for instance. The closer together the walls are, the lower the danger the roof will collapse. The safest place is under a solid table. Enough food should always be kept at home in regions prone to earthquakes.

How many earthquakes are there?

Scientists register up to 100,000 quakes a year. But most of them are so weak that no one notices them.

What is a seismic centre?

A seismic centre is not an earthquake research laboratory, but an earthquake's underground point of origin. The epicentre lies on the surface above it. From here, the dangerous surface shock waves radiate out to encompass the Earth like the circular ripples caused by throwing a stone into a pond. An earthquake is particularly intense near its epicentre.

Have earthquake catastrophes happened in Europe?

Yes. On 1st November 1755, two thirds of Lisbon was destroyed by an earthquake and a flood wave that followed. A devastating fire broke out. Around 20,000 people lost their lives.

Can earthquakes be prevented?

No. But in regions prone to earthquakes, houses are built on flexible foundations that are less susceptible to the shock waves and thereby keep the damage as low as possible.

Snakes leave their holes and hiding places before an earthquake.

Is there always the same amount of rock?

The amount of rock on Earth cannot be reduced, even when mountains are slowly eroded by wind and water. The rock simply changes into sand and rubble, is deposited and can become solid again under pressure. But inside a volcano or when two lithospheric plates meet, all rock can become so hot that it melts.

What types of stone are there?

Magmatic or cooled molten rock is created by lava from a volcanic eruption. Sedimentary rock such as sandstone or limestone is formed by layers of sediment. Metamorphic rock like marble or slate is created when already existing rock finds its way into the Earth's interior and is changed by heat or pressure.

How do flints get their name?

Flint is another name for firestone. It was used in the 17th century to make sparks to set off muskets. Stone Age people could already make knives out of flint. Flint is black or grey inside with a white edge on the outside. It is created by the skeleton remains of crustaceans and plants, and is therefore a sedimentary rock.

Marble is a metamorphic rock.

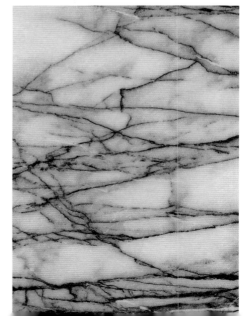

Quartz is a component of many rocks but is also found as a gem, seen here as an amethyst geode in a slab of agate. The crystals are coloured violet by the minerals iron, manganese and titanium.

Slate breaks into plates. That is why it is a good material to use for tiling roofs.

Volcanic glass is an igneous rock. It is formed when lava is catapulted out of a volcano. The lava cools rapidly, forming volcanic glass. Obsidian, for example, has a smooth and glass-like surface. It is very easy to cut oneself on it. But it is only possible to see through very thin plates of obsidian. It is black, dark grey or brownish.

How is volcanic glass created?

School blackboards were formerly made from slate. It is easy to write on it with chalk. Slate breaks into plates and is easy to split. It was therefore easy to make blackboards from it. But woe betide the pupil who pushes another up against a blackboard … Slate is also used to tile roofs.

What were blackboards made of in the past?

Materials that dissolve in water and become stone when the water evaporates are known as natural cements. Lime and silicic acid are two such cements. Conglomerate stone is created when they infiltrate gravel or shingle. Conglomerate stone can be found on former coasts or where glaciers have deposited mountain rubble.

Does cement exist in nature?

Do people today still live in caves?

Stone Age people often lived in caves that offered them shelter. In caves it is never too warm or too cold. It is possible to see winter through in them. Early people used natural caves in which they also painted pictures on the walls. There are still cave villages, although most of them have been dug into soft stone by people. In China for example 40 million people live in underground houses. The individual homes are reached by shafts into the ground. The caves in Cappadocia in Turkey are popular as storehouses. The consistent temperature and humidity allow fruit and vegetables to be stored for a long time.

The area around the Dordogne River in France is well known for its cave systems. Especially famous is the Lascaux grotto in which one of the best preserved examples of prehistoric wall painting can be found.

Where is the world's biggest cave?

The world's biggest cave is the Mammoth Cave in the USA. It has five storeys and a surface area of about 12 square kilometres (4.5 square miles).

What are speleologists?

Speleologists study caves. Some people study caves as an occupation, others as a hobby. They explore caves and measure them with measuring tapes, compasses and clinometers. Then they draw up maps of the individual shafts and caverns. Cave explorers have to be good mountaineers and rock climbers.

Caves are formed in limestone when slightly acidic rainwater slowly dissolves the rock.

Natural caves, such as this one in Arizona in the USA, provide people and animals with shelter from heat and cold.

Is the olm born blind?

The olm lives in complete darkness. It still has eyes and optic nerves in the first weeks of its life, but they completely degenerate over 18 months.

What are ice caves?

An ice cave is formed when the melt water of a glacier has washed away a hollow space in the rock. When the altitude is high enough, the air in the cave stays so cold even in summer that the water freezes. The water that penetrates the cave forms icicles, like limestone stalagmites and stalactites.

How are natural caves created?

Caves form especially often in a karst region, in limestone mountains for instance. Examples in Germany are the Swabian Mountains with around 700 caves, and the Franconian Mountains with 1,200 known caves. Rainwater is always slightly acidic. When this mild acid infiltrates limestone, it gradually dissolves the rock. It creates a system of shafts and caverns. Dripstones can form in the caves. Wafer-thin layers of limestone form when the limy water drips onto the ground from the roof. Over thousands of years stalactites form on the roof and stalagmites on the ground.

Why don't bats fly against the wall in the dark?

The bat practically has a radar system in its body. It transmits sounds at a pitch higher than a person can hear. Bats have such good ears that they can hear the echo and recognise how far away an obstacle is.

Who's nibbling away at the mountain?

The word "erosion" comes from the Latin word "erodere", which translated means "to eat away". We talk of erosion when, over the course of many millions of years, a mountain gets smaller and smaller or a valley deeper and deeper. The causes of erosion are water, wind and ice.

When will the Alps be completely eroded?

That is impossible to predict because the Alps are a very young mountain range that is still growing. The forces of erosion in this region are therefore not as strong as those causing the Alps to grow.

Can erosion be observed?

A human will certainly never see a whole mountain erode. Water, wind and ice work much too slowly for that. But when you see a pebble in a river, it was very probably brought there from the mountains by a river current.

Is erosion the same everywhere?

No. Erosion appears mostly where it rains often and heavily. But stone is also eroded where there are glaciers, where powerful waves break on the shore and where strong winds blow.

This tuff slope has already largely suffered from the forces of erosion.

The effectiveness of erosion also depends on the hardness of the rock. In the Grand Canyon there are alternately hard and soft layers of rock that resist erosion to greater and lesser degrees. That's why the valley slopes look like stairs.

How were the Grand Canyon's stairs created?

Erosion is reduced where the ground is protected by plants. Although it rains a lot, there is not a great deal of erosion in Central Europe because it is covered by relatively dense vegetation.

Where is there little erosion?

Tall Anna ("Lange Anna") is a high, narrow cliff column just off the coast of Helgoland, in Germany. Crashing waves have created this natural piece of art. Tall Anna is supported by artificial concrete barriers to enable tourists to marvel at it for a long time to come.

How long will "Tall Anna" remain standing?

A mushroom rock looks like a giant mushroom but consists of normal rock. Such rocks are created in the desert where the wind carries sand that rubs away the stone like sandpaper.

Is a mushroom rock a petrified mushroom?

In the Grand Canyon in the USA there are alternating hard and soft layers of rock.

Erosion by wind and sand has given the rock its striking appearance.

What do the results of erosion look like?

If you have ever played in a sandpit or built a sandcastle on the beach then you have held the results of erosion in your hands: sand.

How quickly do dunes wander?

A dune is a hill of sand created by the wind. Some dunes can become very large, like the current 137-metre-high (500-foot) Dune du Pylat in France. A dune begins to wander unless sufficiently anchored by vegetation: wind continually carries away grains of sand and changes the dune's position. Sand dunes can move 10 to 20 metres (up to 65 feet) a year, whereby the speed depends on the strength of the wind and the size of the dune. Large dunes wander more slowly than small ones, since more sand must be moved in the case of large dunes.

What is thermal shock?

Thermal shock, also known as onion-skin weathering, happens when there is great heat in the daytime and extreme cold at night, as is the case in the Sahara for example. The fluctuation in temperature breaks down rocks over time. The resulting fine material is usually then carried off by the wind.

Tree roots force their way through the rock surface and thereby prevent erosion.

Wind constantly changes a sand dune's location.

Pigs are often fattened on forage maize. But this plant leaves the soil relatively unprotected allowing fertile soil to be washed away.

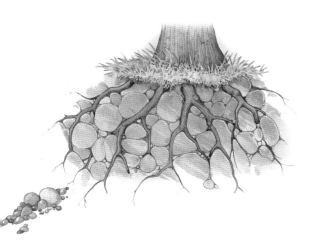

Ice in the form of a glacier certainly has the strength to erode rock. The material it carries along is then deposited many miles away. Where a glacier has retreated and the weather becomes warmer, a hilly landscape of lakes, woods and grassland is left behind.

Can ice also erode rock?

Glaciers usually move along existing river valleys, reshaping them. Such a valley has steep slopes and a trough-like valley floor. It looks like a large U and is therefore also called a U-shaped valley. Another name is trough valley, because the shape is similar to an oversized feeding trough.

How can I recognise a valley formed by a glacier?

Pigs are largely fattened on forage maize. But this plant leaves the fields' soil relatively unprotected. Therefore much fertile soil is washed away, particularly when there is heavy rainfall.

What do pork chops have to do with erosion?

Soil erosion is a big problem worldwide. Agriculture and the rearing of livestock are often the cause. When the population grows, people either migrate to other regions or intensify agricultural production in the areas they already inhabit. In both cases nature is overburdened. In North America deep furrows have been gorged in the ground. The soil in Africa and Asia is being washed away or eroded by the wind.

Is there soil erosion in other countries?

Attempts are made to lessen erosion on steep slopes by ploughing fields parallel to the contour lines. Animals in arid regions should be kept in barns and fed on cut grass. But erosion cannot be completely prevented.

How can people prevent soil erosion?

THE ATMOSPHERE

An atmosphere is the layer of air around a planet. People usually mean the Earth's atmosphere when they speak of the atmosphere. After all, no one has ever been to another planet. The atmosphere protects the Earth from radiation and meteorites from space. It also provides the gases important for sustaining life on Earth: oxygen for people and animals, carbon dioxide for plants. In addition, all weather events also take place in the atmosphere. It is therefore essential for life on Earth, and that is why many people are struggling to protect it.

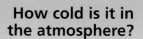
What is the structure of the atmosphere?

The atmosphere consists of several layers, also called spheres. At the bottom is the troposphere. At the poles it reaches up to a height of 50 kilometres (over 30 miles). Above it the mesosphere stretches up to 80 kilometres (50 miles), and above that lies the thermosphere, which ends at about 400 kilometres (250 miles). The outermost layer is the exosphere, which then gives way to the airlessness of space.

How cold is it in the atmosphere?

The temperature in the upper reaches of the troposphere is only -60 °C. But it does not continue like that for the rest of the atmosphere. The temperature initially rises again to 0 °C in the stratosphere. The mesosphere is a layer in which the temperature again sinks until it rises once again to reach over 2,000 °C in the thermosphere.

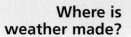
Where is weather made?

The troposphere is the kitchen in which the weather is prepared. Almost all the atmosphere's water can be found as water vapour or cloud in this the lowest layer of the atmosphere. Here horizontal and vertical movements of air occur that as winds bring rain or drought.

Our Earth is covered by a thin atmosphere consisting of several layers. From the bottom to the top they are called: troposphere, stratosphere, mesosphere, thermosphere and exosphere.

Almost all the atmosphere's water can be found as water vapour or clouds in the troposphere, the bottom layer of the atmosphere. Above it stretches the stratosphere with its protective ozone layer.

This is best shown with a comparison. Let's assume that a one kilo bag of sugar represents the weight of all the Earth's water. Then 972 grams would be the water in the oceans and 21.5 grams the water in the Earth's ice. That leaves about 6.5 grams – about a teaspoonful. Of this, 6.2 grams is ground-water. 0.28 grams of the remaining 0.3 grams are stored in lakes and rivers. Only 0.02 grams can be found in the atmosphere as clouds or water vapour. That is the equivalent of a small pinch of sugar.

Which gases make up the air?

The air of the troposphere consists of oxygen, nitrogen, argon, carbon dioxide, and other gases. People and animals need gas to breathe. They exhale carbon dioxide when they breathe out. Plants need carbon dioxide to grow, and thereby produce oxygen. In this way the life forms on Earth complement one another perfectly.

Which layer of the atmosphere protects the skin?

The ozone layer in the lower stratosphere is an important protective shield – ozone is a certain form of oxygen. This layer at a height of 15 to 55 kilometres (about 10 to 35 miles) captures most of the sun's ultraviolet radiation.

Does the Earth have other protective shields?

The Earth's magnetic field creates the magneto-sphere that stretches beyond the atmosphere and protects the Earth from dangerous ionisation radiation from the sun. In addition, clouds reflect short-wave radiation.

How high do weather balloons rise?

Weather balloons fitted with instruments to measure temperature, air pressure, wind speed and collect other data, can rise to about 30 kilometres (19 miles), in good conditions even up to 50 kilometres (30 miles).

What is the colour of air?

The air is a colourless mix of gases. It cannot be seen. But sometimes it is possible to see the many dust particles it contains.

How are the polar lights created?

Polar lights can be seen in both northern and southern Polar Regions (Northern Lights and Southern Lights). They are created by charged particles from space that are diverted to the poles. On their way they cause the atmosphere's gases to glow. Polar lights are usually green and blue in colour and look like a wavy curtain in the sky.

At what altitude do polar lights form?

Polar lights form in the upper layers of the atmosphere at a height of between 100 to 1,000 kilometres (60 to 600 miles). They can be seen well in northern Scandinavia.

Polar lights are created by charged particles from space.

Is the red glow of sunset also caused by particles from space?

No. Glowing sunsets are caused by so-called refraction of the sun's rays. The sun lies very low in the sky at sunset. And so the distance the rays have to travel to reach the person watching the sunset is greater. This filters out the blue and green short-wave segments of sunlight. The observer primarily sees the red and yellow long-wave segments. He sees an orangey-red sunset.

Where do satellites fly?

Some weather satellites, such as ESSA, orbit the Earth at a distance of between 800 to 1,500 kilometres (500 to over 900 miles). Other weather satellites and news satellites fly at a height of 30,000 to 40,000 kilometres (18,600 to 25,000 miles). The Earth's gravity is as strong at this height as the force pulling the satellite out into space, and so it appears from the Earth's surface to stand still in the sky. Such a position is called geostationary.

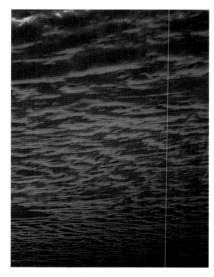

Red sunsets are caused by refraction of the sun's rays through the atmosphere.

Joseph Kittinger didn't jump from a height of 31 kilometres (over 19 miles) for pleasure. It was a test by the American air force to see whether pilots could save themselves with parachutes from a great height. The test was a success but Kittinger almost lost a hand during the flight because a glove was not completely airtight. During his freefall he reached a top speed of 988 km/h (614 mph).

It is difficult to see a satellite from Earth with the naked eye, but it is possible. However, the observer should be at a high location with a dry climate. Satellites differ from shooting stars in as much as they do not burn up and fly more slowly. Neither can they be mistaken for aeroplanes, since they are faster and do not blink.

Can satellites be seen from Earth?

The big jets that take people on holidays mostly fly at a height of 10 to 20 kilometres (6 to 12 miles). This brings them above the turbulent troposphere. This has the advantage that the passengers do not feel sick as quickly.

How high do passenger jets fly?

A hot-air balloon always travels only at the same speed as the air current in which it finds itself. That's why we sometimes speak of a balloon ride instead of a balloon flight. And by the way: hot-air balloons were the very first vehicles for flying. The first successful flight in a balloon, the Montgolfiere, took place in Paris on 21.11.1783.

Is a balloon journey a flight or a ride?

In 1960 the American Joseph Kittinger jumped out of the basket of a helium-filled balloon. He was 31 kilometres (over 19 miles) above the Earth, in the stratosphere. No one has yet broken his record.

How high was the highest human parachute jump?

The Asian bar-headed goose holds the animal kingdom's record for altitude. It breads in Central Asia but spends the winter in India. On its journey south from its breeding ground the goose has to fly over the Himalayas. In doing so it achieves a flight altitude of up to 8 kilometres (5 miles).

Which animal holds the altitude record?

A hot-air balloon always flies with the air current.

What is a climate?

A climate is the characteristic situation of the atmosphere near the surface of a particular region. The air temperature, rainfall, wind strength and other data have to be collected over several decades in order to determine the climate of a region. When this data is complete, it is possible to know roughly which months are best for taking a bathing holiday in the region in question. But it is not possible to predict how the weather will be on every day of the holiday.

How is air temperature measured?

With a thermometer. But to ensure the measurement is not falsified by direct sunshine or the warming effect of the ground or house walls, the thermometer is placed in a shaded location between 1.2 and 2 metres (4 and 6 ½ feet) above the ground.

Why is it warmer at the Equator than at the Poles?

The cause is the Earth's round shape. The sun's rays always hit the Earth's surface at the Equator at a much steeper angle than at the Poles. The sun's heat is therefore concentrated on a smaller surface area than at the Poles, where the same amount of solar energy has to heat a much wider surface. This is why it is much colder there.

Amsterdam has a maritime climate because the city lies so close to the sea.

A caravan along a desert trail in the Sahara: here the highest temperature of 58 °C was measured.

Starting at the Equator, the four major climatic zones are the Tropics, the Subtropics, the Temperate Zones and the Polar Regions. These groups are themselves sub-divided according to rainfall, the annual distribution of rainfall and other benchmarks.

How many different climates are there?

Starting at the Equator and finishing at the Poles, the four major climatic zones are the Tropics, the Subtropics, the Temperate Zones and the Polar Regions. These groups are themselves sub-divided according to rainfall, the annual distribution of rainfall and other benchmarks.

Why does it snow more often in Berlin than in Amsterdam?

It snows more often in Berlin although both cities are just as far from the North Pole. The reason is that Amsterdam lies nearer the sea. Its climate is known as "maritime" in contrast to a "continental" climate with hot summers and cold winters.

Which is the world's coldest climate?

Greenland and the Antarctic are subject to an ice climate. There the temperature only climbs above 0 °C during the short summer, if at all. The lowest temperature ever recorded was also measured in the Antarctic: -89 °C.

Where was the highest temperature measured?

The highest temperature of 58 °C was measured on the edge of the Sahara in Libya, North Africa. It is essential that anyone who travels there take a sunhat and lots of drinking water.

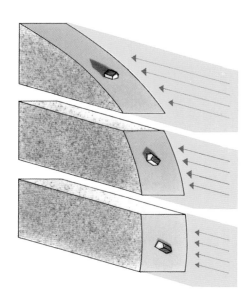

What are clouds made of?

Clouds are made up of very small drops of water and ice crystals. There are clouds made up purely of water drops, clouds of only ice crystals and mixed clouds. Low hanging clouds usually consist of droplets of water, those much higher up of ice crystals.

How do clouds form?

Clouds form when air rises. The air cools when it rises. The invisible water vapour in the air then turns into small droplets of water. This process is called condensation.

Do all clouds bring rain?

No. Many clouds dissolve before they bring rain or snow. Then the water droplets and ice crystals turn back into gaseous water vapour. This process is called evaporation, and can be seen when the puddles on the road slowly disappear after a summer rain shower.

Do skyscrapers really reach up into the clouds?

Some clouds hang so low that the top of a 500-metre-high skyscraper can disappear in them. But no building by man can reach the upper limit of the clouds, which lies at a height of around 15 kilometres (9 miles).

*Lightening flashes across the sky!
An enormous amount of energy is
released by an electrical discharge.*

*Cotton-wool clouds belong to the cumulus
type of cloud: against a radiant blue sky
they are usually a sign of good weather.*

Feather-like clouds, known as cirrus, form in the sky at great height.

What types of clouds are there?

Clouds are divided into the two general categories of layered clouds (stratus) and convective clouds (cumulus). Stratus clouds form a complete blanket of cloud, while cumulus clouds can be seen individually.

To which type of cloud do cotton-wool clouds belong?

Cotton-wool clouds are cumulus clouds. Individual clouds can be clearly identified. Some look like balls of cotton-wool or woolly sheep. These are also commonly known as fine-weather clouds because they are a sign of fine weather to come.

What is struck on a "storm anvil"?

Storm clouds that stretch high up into the sky are called storm anvils because their tops are flattened giving them the appearance of a blacksmith's anvil. They are the highest clouds. In central Europe they reach a height of 6 to 12 kilometres (4 to 8 miles), and up to 18 kilometres (11 miles) at the Equator. Of course, nothing is struck on these clouds, but strong storms can brew up in them.

How are thunder and lightening created?

Friction between the droplets of water and ice crystals in a storm cloud creates an electrical charge. The upper part of the cloud becomes positively charged and the lower part negatively. An electrical discharge occurs when the charge reaches a certain strength and then lightening flashes across the sky. The energy released heats up the surrounding air in a split second. The air expands faster than the speed of sound, causing the sound of thunder.

How is rain created?

Rain occurs when the tiny droplets of water in a cloud join together to form increasingly larger drops. Sooner or later the drops are so big that the air can no longer carry them. They fall to Earth as rain drops.

How is rainfall measured?

To measure how much rain has fallen in a particular spot, the falling rain is caught and channelled into a container. The amount of rainfall is then measured in millimetres. In Essen, in Germany for example, an average of 829 millimetres of rain falls every year.

Where does it rain most?

The record is held by a weather station on the peak of Wai-ale-ali on Kauai, a Hawaiian island. An annual average of 15,000 millimetres of rain falls there. That's 15 metres of rain!

What is dew?

Dew forms over night. The air cools and the water vapour it contains condenses on the cold surfaces of plants and the ground. You can see dew in spiders' webs, for example, when you go outside early in the morning. But it then evaporates very quickly.

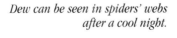

Dew can be seen in spiders' webs after a cool night.

Raindrops pouring down.

Fog itself cannot be caught because, like clouds, it is made up of very fine droplets of water. But these droplets are indeed collected in dry regions in which fog or mist often occurs. Nets are hung out on which the droplets are deposited. Some water for irrigating the fields is won this way on the Pacific coast of South America.

Can fog be captured?

Hailstones form in high cumulonimbus clouds. Small ice crystals are carried up into the cloud by the circulating air currents. More and more rings of ice form around them like the skins of an onion. Sooner or later they become too heavy and fall to Earth. Hail storms are feared by farmers in particular because they can cause an enormous amount of damage.

How are hail-stones created?

Where we live hailstones are usually no bigger than marbles. But in Bangladesh, in Asia, hailstones as big as a man's fist and weighing a kilogram have been observed.

How big can hail-stones become?

Fog and mist are made up of very fine droplets of water.

What are snowflakes made of?

Snowflakes are made up of very fine ice crystals that have grown on to one another. They fall to Earth as snow when they become too heavy. But often they melt before reaching the ground. Then they reach us as raindrops.

Why do winds exist?

Winds are currents of air between areas of high air pressure and areas of low air pressure. The weight of the air at a certain place is called the air pressure. This weight is not the same everywhere. Winds try to balance out these differences in pressure, and blow from areas of high pressure to areas of low pressure. The air is heated most strongly at the Equator. It expands and becomes "thinner", the air pressure falls. Air then flows in from areas with higher air pressure.

How fast are winds?

The highest wind speed ever measured on Earth was 371 kilometres an hour (230 mph). That's roughly the highest speed achieved during a Formula One race. Winds are much slower as a rule. But they can still cause minor damage at 80 kilometres an hour (50 mph).

Snowflakes are made up of ice crystals that have grown on to one another.

Most tornadoes occur in the south of the USA and often cause great damage.

Wind is needed for wind surfing. Winds are currents of air between areas of high air pressure and areas of low air pressure.

Hurricanes form over very warm seawater of at least 26.5 °C. The moist air warms up and rapidly rises in a spiral-like movement around the centre of the hurricane. In doing so it cools and dense clouds are formed that can reach up to 12 kilometres (7 ½ miles) in height.

How are hurricanes created?

If it could see it would look out onto a cloudless sky because in the centre of a hurricane – its eye – the wind is almost still and no clouds form there. It would usually see the sea below because it quickly breaks up when it makes its way inland where the moisture it needs is missing. Nevertheless, hurricanes often cause terrible damage.

What can a hurricane see with its eye?

Tornadoes are very small whirlwinds that usually last for only a few minutes. They often occur in the American states of Texas and Illinois, where in summer warm moist air from the Gulf of Mexico meets dry cold air from the Rocky Mountains. This difference causes tornadoes to form. On average, 750 tornadoes occur in the USA every year. Whirlwinds are seldom seen in Europe.

Where do most tornadoes occur?

People who go searching for tornadoes are called tornado hunters in the USA. Their "weapons" are photographic equipment and video cameras.

What weapons are used by tornado hunters?

A monsoon is a tropical wind. It is most pronounced in South and Southeast Asia and on the East African coast. The monsoon is a constant wind that changes its direction every six months. In India and large areas of Asia it is responsible for heavy rainfall in summer. In winter it blows from the north and is dry.

Where does the monsoon blow?

THE OCEANS

Two thirds of the Earth's surface is covered by the sea. The three big oceans are the Pacific, the Atlantic and the Indian Oceans. In the south the three come together to form the South Polar Ocean, in the north they form the North Polar Ocean. 97 per cent of the Earth's water is found in the oceans. A range of plants and animals are at home here, most of them near the coasts. But there is also life in the open seas and on the seabed. A lot of people like to go on holiday to the seaside. Fish and other seafood provide an important source of food for people. Even drinking water can be won in desalination plants.

How much salt is in one cubic metre of seawater?

Approximately 35 kilograms of salt is dissolved in one cubic metre of seawater, that's about two bathtubs filled to the brim. The salt content is a little less in rainy areas of the sea, and higher in hot, dry ones. The salt was already present when the Earth was formed, but was overwhelmingly to be found in rock. Rainfall washed it out of the rock and transported it into the sea through rivers and streams.

One cubic metre of seawater contains around 35 kilograms of salt. It was washed out of the Earth's rocks by rainwater.

How warm is the oceans' water?

The temperature at the water surface ranges from -2 °C to 35 °C. Then the water is as warm as the water in a bathtub. 20 °C is already a pleasant temperature for swimming. The sun warms the water most at the Equator. But even there the sun's rays are not strong enough to reach the seabed. Near the Equator, it is bitterly cold at depths more than 1,000 metres (3,200 feet) under the sea surface. The temperature doesn't rise above 5 °C. The average temperature of the oceans lies under 4 °C.

Is there also life in the frozen Polar Oceans?

The icefish of the Antarctic don't die even when they are frozen in ice. Their thin, pale blood without red blood cells contains glycoprotein that only freezes in very low temperatures.

Water is lighter in colour near land. The next coast is also not far away when a lot of birds can be seen circling the ship. Cumulus clouds on the horizon are a sign of an island or the mainland.

How can you tell from onboard ship that land is near?

The Pacific Ocean's name is derived from the Spanish or Portuguese word "Pacifico", which means "peaceful". It was so named by the Portuguese sailor Ferdinand Magellan because the wind was favourable when he sailed around the world in 1521. The Pacific is the largest ocean.

Where does the name „Pacific Ocean" derive from?

Turtles spend most of their lives in the open sea and come onto the beach only to lay their eggs.

The high sea is not as rich in nutrition as coastal areas. More phytoplankton grows near the coast. Those are small algae that provide food for fish. The algae need sunlight and so cannot flourish as well in deep water. Fewer animal species live in the open sea: jellyfish, squid, crabs, turtles and fish, but also mammals such as dolphins, whales and seals.

Why do fewer animals live in the open sea than near the coast?

It is dark in the depths of the sea, and the water is cold. Nevertheless, several animals still live more than 1,000 metres (3,200 feet) below the sea surface. Some species of deep-sea animals have light-producing organs for orientation. Lanternfish for example are equipped with glowing bands along their bodies. The anglerfish has a lantern in front of its jaws with which it attracts its prey.

Who glows in the sea depths?

In the South Seas long cords full of oysters are placed in the sea. Small stones are purposely put into the mussels' shells and then coated by the animals with a smooth, shiny material. The resulting pearls can be harvested after about two years.

Is the sea also harvested?

Why do high and low tides occur?

The sea level on most of the Earth's coasts rises and falls twice a day. The length of time between one high-water mark and the next is twelve hours and 25 minutes. So it's possible to go swimming in the North Sea 50 minutes later every day. This is due to the movement of the moon. It takes 24 hours and 50 minutes to circle the Earth once. The Earth and the moon attract one another. That is why the oceans' water aligns itself according to the moon. The moon pulls a tide of water with it as it circles the Earth.

How does the sun interfere?

The sun also exerts a pulling force on the Earth and the water of the oceans. But its effect is much less than that of the moon. The sun does, however, cause spring tides to occur every two months. That is always the case when the sun and the moon stand exactly behind each other as seen from the Earth. The forces of attraction of both the sun and the moon combine and the tide rises especially high.

The Earth and moon attract one another, causing high and low tides along the Earth's coasts.

What is the tidal range?

The difference between flood at high tide and ebb at low tide is called the tidal range. The tidal range on the open Atlantic coast is around two to three metres (six to ten feet).

Why is it possible to swim in the Mediterranean throughout the day?

The difference between high and low tide on the Mediterranean coast is very slight. The tidal range here is less than a metre. This is because the water can flow into the ocean only through the narrow Straits of Gibraltar. This slows down the water as it follows the moon's movement. That is why it is possible to swim in the Mediterranean throughout the day. The water cannot flow so easily out of the Baltic Ocean either, which is why the difference between high and low tide is also slight here.

The difference between high and low tide in the Mediterranean is only slight. That's why coastal towns need no sea walls to protect them from flooding.

The term mean sea level (MSL for short) is used to describe a fixed value for determining altitudes on the Earth's surface. A location's altitude is given as metres or feet "above mean sea level" or AMSL. It is necessary to fix mean sea level because the height of sea level varies due to the tides. For example the altitude for Saarbrucken in Germany was different when measured from the Atlantic than when measured from the North Sea.

Many animals find rich food in the mudflats of the German North Sea coast.

What is a mudflat?

Mudflats are especially flat areas of coast where the sea has deposited much sand and mud. A 10-to-20-kilometre (6-to-12-mile) wide strip is laid dry at low tide. The water flows away to the open sea through channels. The German North Sea coast is a mudflat called the Wadden Sea.

What animals live in and on mudflats?

Little piles of mud that look like string can be seen when walking over mudflats. These are the faeces of lugworms that filter algae out of the mud. Up to a million algae live in a thimbleful of mud. Sandhoppers and laver spire shell snails can be found in enormous quantities. Together with washed-up jellyfish, polyps and starfish, they provide food for birds. Terns breed on the islands of the North Sea and Baltic Ocean.

What is a holm?

A holm is a small rounded islet. There are ten inhabited holms off the coast of Schleswig-Holstein in Germany. The best-known is called Hallig Hooge. The houses stand on earthen mounds to protect them from flooding.

What is a tidal power station?

A tidal power station produces electricity by using the energy of the water currents flowing between high and low tides. Tidal power stations are built on sea bays with an especially high tidal range. The bays are dammed by a dyke to force the water through the turbines.

What is a storm surge?

A storm surge is a high tide in which the sea level is heightened by wind blowing inland. A devastating storm surge in 1962 claimed many victims in Germany and Denmark.

Do waves transport my message in a bottle?

Waves only appear to transport water and other objects. In reality, the waves glide through under the bottle. One moment the bottle finds itself at the crest of a wave, then it falls down into the wave's trough. The water turns in circles and the bottle only makes progress with a steady wind. Once the message has slowly and leisurely made its way toward the coast it moves a bit more quickly. The wave troughs, in the surf are quicker than the wave crests, which are slowed down by rubbing on the ever shallower seabed. The waves break and throw the bottle onto the shore.

How is it possible to avoid becoming seasick?

Seasickness is caused by the rocking motion of the waves. The balance organs become irritated, causing nausea. Waves are felt less in the middle of a ship.

How is a whirlpool created?

Whirlpools or vortices are created when ocean currents meet. That is often the case in straits, stretches of water between islands or landmasses. Charybdis' whirlpools in the Straits of Messina, between Italy and Sicily, also played a role in ancient Greek sagas.

Tsunamis are the most dangerous waves. They can tower up to a height of 80 metres (260 feet) when they reach the shore.

Currents are often driven by seas that are almost cut off from the rest of the ocean. More water evaporates from the Mediterranean than flows into it. The salty water sinks into the depths and is pushed through the Straits of Gibraltar in a strong current. Less salty Atlantic water flows back into the Mediterranean above the salty water pouring into the ocean. This movement of water is called compensation current.

What drives seawater around the world?

The Gulf Stream is a current flowing between the Gulf of Mexico and Europe. It ensures a mild climate in northwestern Europe.

How can palm trees grow in England?

Tsunamis are the most dangerous waves. They are created by earthquakes on the seabed. The waves are lower and innocuous on the open sea, but then pile up to 80 metres (260 feet) high at the coast where they sweep away everything in their path.

How are the most dangerous waves created?

El Niño (Spanish for "little boy" and referring to the Christ child) is a very warm sea current that sometimes occurs off the northwest coast of South America at around Christmas time. Great numbers of fish, birds and corals then die.

What is El Niño?

Waves break on the shore because they are obstructed by the ever shallower seabed.

The best place to be in case of seasickness is the middle of the ship. There the rocking motion can be felt the least.

Is the seabed even?

The seabed is just as uneven as the continents. Mountain ranges can be found in the middle of all large oceans, the so-called ridges. They are several thousand kilometres long. Magma swells up from inside the Earth at the ridges and forces the mountain ranges apart. There are also deep trenches in the seabed. With a depth of more than 11,000 metres (36,000 feet), the Marianna Trench between the Pacific and the Philippine plates is the deepest.

Is pillow lava especially soft?

Pillow lava is so called because it looks like sofa pillows. Volcanoes beneath the sea surface spew out lava just like those on land. But the lava hardens rapidly in the cool ocean water. Lava pillows are large, cooled drops of lava.

Black smokers provide food and warmth for many animals of the deep sea.

Where do blind white crabs live?

Sometimes hot springs shoot through the Earth's crust near volcanic mountains on the deep-sea bed. The water they spew out is black and looks like a column of smoke. It contains a lot of minerals leached out of the volcanic rock. Because bacteria feed on minerals, blind white crabs, various types of fish and tube worms also find something to eat.

The island of Iceland lies on the Atlantic deep-sea ridge.

Not only the fauna and flora of our oceans fascinate divers. A shipwreck is always a spectacular find.

What colour is the seabed?

The red mud in the estuaries of several tropical rivers contains so much iron sulphate that it colours the seabed red. Green mud can be found off the Spanish and Portuguese Atlantic coast. Yellow diatom mud consists of the cell walls of diatom algae and covers the seabed around the Antarctic.

Why are sandbanks so dangerous for ships?

Sandbanks often consist of loose quicksand. When a ship misses the navigation channel and hits the sand it can sink into it. Even a tugboat might then fail to pull the ship back out.

In Iceland a deep-sea ridge can be seen on the surface. The island lies exactly on top of the Atlantic deep-sea ridge, where the Eurasian and North American plates border one another. The middle of the island is made up of volcanoes. And on Iceland it is just the same as on deep-sea ridges under water: the further away from the middle of the mountain, the older the basalt rock.

Sonar is the English abbreviation of "Sound Navigation and Ranging". The method was invented around 1920. A sonar is also called an echo sounder, because the device sends sound waves into the water and then records their echoes. This way, information about the composition of the seabed can be gathered and maps produced. Sonar systems are also used in fishing for tracking down and determining the size of shoals of fish.

Are there deep-sea ridges on the mainland?

What is a sonar?

LANDSCAPES

Landscape is the term used for a geographic area that is distinguished from other areas through its special form or temperatures. This is how deserts and arid areas, forests and grasslands are differentiated from coastal and island landscapes. There are also mountain landscapes, river and lake landscapes as well as the Polar Regions. Each landscape provides a home for different species of animals and plants through its special climatic conditions. Only humans can live in almost every landscape: they cross the hottest deserts, settle on islands and coasts, and even live in the Arctic and Antarctic.

Are deserts always made of sand?

We usually think of sand when we hear the word desert. But sand makes up only a fifth of the surface of even the world's largest desert, the Sahara. Mountains of more than 3,000 metres (10,000 feet) hight and wide, stony landscapes can also be found there. The world's largest sand desert is therefore not the Sahara, but the Rub' al Khali on the Arabian Peninsula. "Rub' al Khali" means "Empty Quarter" in English.

What are watering holes in the desert called?

A place in the desert where a watering hole or a spring can be found is called an oasis. There are small oases consisting of only a pool and date palms, and very large oases where whole towns are located.

What is the ideal desert house?

Humans have settled in oases and on the edges of the deserts, people like the Berbers of Morocco. They have built towers in which to live. The rooms have tiny windows on the outside. It is always very dark inside because little light penetrates the interior. The rooms therefore remain pleasantly cool. It makes sense in the desert to live high up, because the further away from the ground, the cooler it is. When the ground surface of the desert is 75 °C, hot enough to burn the soles of the feet, the temperature at a height of 20 metres (65 feet) is only 26 °C.

Only a fifth of the Sahara is covered with sand.

It is not always hot in the desert. Daytime and nighttime temperatures vary greatly. It can still freeze at night even when it's 50 °C hot during the day. This is because the desert is not as well insulated as, for example, a wood that retains the warm air. Another of the Earth's insulation layers is clouds, which are normally missing over the desert. And incidentally, it's not a bad idea to wear an anorak in the midday heat, too. It also protects against heat, and not just cold. A Tuareg, a desert nomad, doesn't remove the cloth wound around his head even when eating.

Why should you take a thick anorak with you in the desert?

Old deserts such as the Namib Desert in southern Africa have been barren for a very long time. But some areas of the Sahara and the Gobi Desert were moist enough 5,000 to 8,000 years ago for crops to be grown and livestock raised there.

Were deserts always so desert-like?

The acacia's roots burrow to an enormous depth to reach groundwater. The roots are sometimes much longer than the tree's trunk. The acacia is known as an indicator species because it shows where groundwater is available.

How does the acacia get its water?

Loose sand offers little resistance, so snakes find insufficient hold for their belly scales. They therefore twist their bodies into several consecutive S curves. Only in this way can they heave themselves off the ground. This type of movement is called side-winding.

Why do desert snakes move sideways?

Caravans are large groups of merchants who even during the 20th century crossed the deserts of the Middle East and North Africa, mostly using ancient caravan trails. These groups often had more than 1,000 camels to carry their goods.

How were goods transported across the desert in the past?

The houses in the Moroccan desert are built quite high to ensure that their living areas are as far from the ground as possible.

Is it possible to drown in the desert?

Time after time, tourists drown while travelling through the desert. In some areas it rains only every hundred years. But when rain falls, it is usually in great amounts over a very short time. In a rock desert, the water runs off the surface instead of soaking into the ground. Torrential rivers can flow within only a few minutes, and lakes form in the stony landscape.

Are there flowers in the desert?

Some areas of the desert turn into a colourful sea of flowers when rain has fallen. Small flowers sprout within hours and cover the ground as far as the eye can see. They sow their seeds and quickly dry out. They then survive as seeds or bulbs for many years – until the next rain. Another plant, the Rose of Jericho, curls up into a fist-like ball during periods of drought and falls into a dry stasis.

What age can a giant cactus reach?

The Sonora Desert in the southwest of the USA is the home of the giant cactus, also known as the Saguaro or candelabra cactus. It can reach an age of more than 300 years, and a height of 15 metres (50 feet).

Goats contribute to the growth of deserts. When grazing, they tear out herbs with the roots.

When you turn over a stone in the desert you will often find it is completely green underneath. The growth looks like tiny moss. These are lichen and algae that prefer to live under light-coloured and translucent rocks.

Are there algae in the desert?

The Earth's deserts, for example the Sahara, are continually growing. People chop down trees and bushes because they need wood for burning. They also keep goats that eat the few plants, including the roots. Existing water is often used for the fields, preventing it from reaching the streams.

Can deserts grow?

The desert gecko of the Namib Desert burrows its way into the sand during the day. Although the surface of the sand is 75 °C in the heat of the day, it is only 43 °C at a depth of 25 centimetres (10 inches). The ground also protects it.

Who plays hide and seek in the desert?

Sometimes, cold and hot layers of air lay very close to one anther in the desert. They then act as a mirror where they meet. The sky for example is then reflected, creating the optical illusion of a watery surface.

What exactly is a mirage?

Some deserts like this one, Wadi Rum in Jordan, consist mainly of stone. Torrential rivers then form when rain falls.

The giant cactus is also callde candelabra cactus because it looks like a candelabrum.

Why do deciduous trees in Europe shed their leaves in autumn?

In Europe, the temperature in winter sinks below 0 °C and water freezes. Trees can no longer absorb moisture through their roots. To save water during these months they shed their leaves. The loss through evaporation would be too great because the leaves have a very thin skin. In addition, snow can find little room to settle on bare branches. If snow were to settle on the leaves, its weight might break the branches.

Did our woods always look like they do today?

The natural population of our woods is a mixture of deciduous and coniferous trees. Around 1800 there were still two deciduous trees for every conifer. The ratio today is somewhat different. Because the timber industry needs a lot of trees, people have planted mainly coniferous trees, which grow faster than most deciduous trees.

Which is the world's largest tree?

The highest known tree in the world is a sequoia with a height of 112 metres (367 feet). It stands in the Redwood National Park in California. The thickest tree in the world is also a sequoia, called "General Sherman". Its trunk has a circumference of 31.3 metres (over 102 feet). It can be found in the Sequoia National Park in California.

Deciduous and coniferous trees stand alongside one another in a mixed forest.

Deciduous trees in Europe shed their leaves in autumn.

It is hot and humid in rainforests such as this one in Costa Rica.

Alternating rings can be seen on sawn-off tree stumps: some wide, some narrow. They are known as annual rings because every year the tree trunk grows thicker by a ring. The rings are created by the vegetation growing period – the tree grows in summer but not in winter. It is possible to determine the age of a tree by counting its rings. That cannot be done with trees in a tropical rainforest because the climatic conditions are constant and no rings are created.

Why do our trees have rings and those in the tropics do not?

Colourful macaw parrots and loud howler monkeys can be seen in zoos. But few animals – apart from giant ants, leeches and mosquitoes – are likely to be seen in tropical rainforests themselves although more species are at home here than anywhere else on Earth. Many of the mammals live in the trees and hide among the treetops, like, for example, the sloth. In addition, two out of every three species are only active at night. Most creatures are also excellently camouflaged. They blend into their surroundings perfectly and are overlooked when passed by.

Where is the best place to observe jungle animals?

Only on the banks of lakes and rivers, alongside settlements and in clearings, does the green foliage reach to the ground, giving the appearance of an impenetrable wall. Here low-growing plants also get enough light, but deeper inside the rainforest the ground is far less overgrown because sunlight cannot penetrate through the foliage.

Is the rainforest impenetrable?

Two thirds of the world's rainforests can be found in the Amazon Basin in South America. There are also rainforests in Southeast Asia, on New Guinea and in Australia, as well as in Central Africa.

Where are the most rainforests?

What is the difference between steppes and savannas?

Both steppes and savannas are grasslands. Savannas lie in the tropics where the difference in temperature between summer and winter is not great. Instead, there are rainy and arid seasons. Steppes on the other hand can be found in temperate zones. It is cold in winter and only 200 to 500 millimetres of rain fall annually. That is why it is too dry for trees.

Why is it necessary to be a fast runner on the steppes and savannas?

Pronghorn antelope and bison live on the prairies of North America, and lamas on the pampas of South America. In the past, there were also large herds of wild horses on the steppes of Central Asia. Because no bushes grow on the grassland to provide cover, animals have to be good runners to survive. For their hunters are also fast: lions, cheetahs and hyenas chase the gnu and antelope herds until they succeed in killing an animal that is too slow.

Gnus live on the savannas of Africa in large herds.

Which animal can run the fastest?

Cheetahs are the animal kingdom's fastest runners. These big cats with tan-coloured fur covered in dark spots can briefly achieve speeds of up to 100 kilometres per hour (over 60 mph).

How does an anteater eat ants?

Anteaters are at home in the grasslands of Central and South America. They track down colonies of ants and termites with their fine noses and then tear them apart with their big claws. The anteater's tongue is 60 centimetres long (24 inches) and can shoot out up to 150 times a minute to lick up insects.

Elephants like to cool themselves down at waterholes or fan themselves with their ears.

How did the rattlesnake get its name?

If a rattlesnake feels threatened it first warns its attacker with a rattling sound made with the dry rings of horn on the tip of its tail. This characteristic gave the rattlesnake its name. This extremely poisonous animal lives on the prairies of the USA.

The world's largest birds live in grassland regions: the ostrich in South Africa, the nandu in South America and the emu in Australia. They have all forgotten how to fly! Instead they are very fast on foot. The ostrich breaks all records. Weighing up to 150 kilograms and up to three metres (about 10 feet) in height, it is the biggest bird of all. It can reach a speed of 65 kilometres an hour (40 mph).

Why do African elephants have such big ears?

The African elephant needs its ears not just to hear with. The large skin surface helps water to evaporate, cooling the animal's body. Animals in cold regions, like the polar bear, are built more compactly. They have a small body surface in comparison to their weight, so that as little warmth as possible is lost. Animals of the steppes and savannas, by contrast, often have extra large skin surfaces to lose heat. Elephants continually flap their ears and create a breeze. Indian elephants have smaller ears because they can protect themselves from the sun under trees. But trees are rare in the habitat of the African elephant.

Lions hunt their prey in grasslands.

Where can one hide in the grass?

In the rainy season, the grass of the wet savannas of Brazil, the Orinoco in Venezuela and in Central Africa grows as high as a full-grown person. One can therefore hide well in the grass. Savannas are landscapes in which it rains a great deal, but in which not a drop of rain may fall for two to fives months of the year. The grass then dries up and the trees shed their leaves.

Where was the largest prairie?

The largest prairie stretched north from Texas in the US Mid-West to Canada. Large herds of buffalo roamed here before the Europeans came. Very little of the original grassland is left today. Farmers ploughed up the land in the 19th century and began to sow wheat.

Where exactly are the pampas?

In common speech we use the word pampas for an area where nothing happens and no large town is nearby. The real pampas are large grass-covered plains in Argentina, Uruguay and Brazil. They are bordered by the Andes to the west and the Atlantic to the east.

Why is a rain-coat needed more often in Borkum than in Vienna?

The water of the seas functions as a sort of heat buffer. It stays milder on the coast and offshore islands of zones in which it is cold inland in winter. Where there are hot summers inland, it remains pleasantly cool along the sea coast. With only a few exceptions, it is also wetter and windier along the coast and on North Sea islands like Borkum than places inland such as Vienna.

Would Vikings today recognise the coastlines they once knew well?

They would presumably not believe their eyes were they to see the concrete harbour breakwaters. But the coast also changes without human help. Steep coasts are usually a sign that the sea is attacking the land. Waves crash on the rocks with great force until they break off and the land recedes. In other places, the sea deposits rock debris on the beach and the land grows.

How do people gain land from the sea?

In earlier times, the Dutch pumped the water from the land with the help of windmills. This is how man gained fertile land from the ocean. Electric pumps do the work today. Dykes prevent the water from flooding back.

Steep cliffs are washed away by the sea. The land surface recedes. The sea then deposits pebbles and sand on flat shores. The land surface grows.

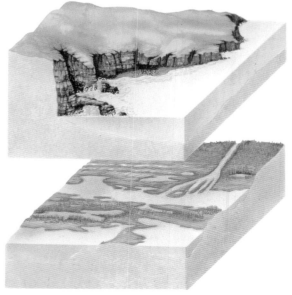

The Brazilian city of Rio de Janeiro lies on the coast. It has almost ten million inhabitants.

All three are major coastal cities. Many people have settled on coasts. Half the world's population lives no further than 80 kilometres (50 miles) away from the sea. Harbours attract people with the possibility for work.

What do Tokyo, New York and Rio de Janeiro have in common?

Coasts appear on satellite pictures as chains of light. Places along the coast can be seen as bright points. This is because so many people live on the coast.

What do coasts look like from above at night?

The towns and villages along the coast need a lot of water, but seawater cannot be drunk. It is too salty. Desalination plants are needed to turn seawater into drinking water. When water is heated and condenses it loses the salt. But only rich countries like those on the Persian Gulf can afford this process.

Can you drink seawater?

The Apostles are twelve high columns of rock off the south coast of Australia. These columns once were a part of a headland that has been washed away almost completely by the sea.

Where are the Apostles?

The land recedes on steep coasts where it is attacked by the sea.

Are islands still being created?

Yes. One of the youngest is the island of Surtsey near Iceland. Fishermen discovered smoke on the water in 1965. They thought that a ship was possibly in difficulty. But they were actually seeing the creation of an island. A volcano had formed underwater and was now reaching the sea surface. Many specialists were astounded to find the first lichens already growing there in 1970, when it was just five years old. More than 100 species of insects were already living there, too. Species of plants and animals can develop undisturbed on islands. 89 per cent of Hawaii's plant species are endemic, which means that they can be found nowhere else.

Some underwater volcanoes pile up so much lava that islands are created.

Why do some islands have black sandy beaches?

Volcanic islands, such as Tahiti, often have black sandy beaches. The sand is created from black volcanic rock, basalt. Hot lava cools down very quickly when it flows into the sea. Sea and waves grind the rock to fine black sand.

How many islands belong to Indonesia?

Indonesia lies in Southeast Asia. The world's largest island state consists of 14,000 islands, which stretch for more than 5,000 kilometres (3,000 miles) from west to east.

Many tropical fish can be observed on coral reefs where they search for food.

Many of the plants on Hawaii can be found nowhere else apart from these Pacific islands.

Where is the world's smallest island state?

With only 10,000 inhabitants and a surface of 21 square kolometres (8 square miles), Nauru in the Pacific is the smallest island state.

Where do corals feel at home?

Corals love warm, tropical seawater from 20°C. They are small animals that cannot move around on their own. Instead they have a firm framework for protection. They live in gigantic colonies and sweep algae into their mouths with their tentacles. Corals can only live in oxygen-rich water near the surface. The seabed would be too dark for them.

When corals die they leave behind a calcium skeleton. New corals settle on this. Over time, the coral constructions reach the sea surface. There they form so-called fringing reefs and over time even atolls. Lagoons can be found in the middle of coral islands, lakes separated from the sea by coral banks. Divers love coral reefs. Many tropical fish can be observed on them. The largest coral reef is the Great Barrier Reef, which stretches for more than 2,000 kilometres (1,200 miles) off the northeastern coast of Australia.

Yes, but a microscope is necessary. Desert sand has round grains of equal size because they are blown by the wind and rubbed together. In the sea there is always water between the grains of sand. They don't rub together directly and are therefore of various sizes and less rounded.

What do coral cemeteries look like?

Can beach sand be differentiated from desert sand?

Do polar bears eat penguins?

No penguin has to be afraid of polar bears, because they're far away. Penguins live in the southern hemisphere, particularly in the Antarctic, and polar bears in the Arctic.

What is the difference between the Arctic and the Antarctic?

The region around the North Pole, the Arctic, is a frozen ocean basin that is 5,300 metres (17,000 feet) at its deepest point. The area around the South Pole, the Antarctic, is a continent the highest mountain of which is 5,140 metres (16,800 feet) high. The ice of the North Polar Ocean is on average no thicker than one to three metres (3 to 12 feet), while the average ice cover of the Antarctic is 1,700 metres (5,600 feet).

Is it always snowing in the Antarctic?

It almost never snows in the Antarctic. The average annual snowfall inland amounts to only five centimetres (2 inches). So a whole year's snowfall would not be enough for skiing.

Who hatches the Emperor's egg?

It's the father who hatches the egg of the Emperor Penguin. The mother comes back only when the offspring has hatched, and packs it into her pouch. The father then has time to recover.

Polar bears live in the Arctic.

Icebergs are made of freshwater. They are not formed in the sea, but have split from glaciers. Glaciers of solid snow and ice make their way from the icecaps of the Northern and Southern Polar Regions towards the sea. Large blocks of ice break off when they come into contact with the water. The glacier is then said to calve. Many icebergs are then carried southward or northward by the sea currents. It takes about three years for an iceberg to melt on the open sea.

Are icebergs made of frozen seawater?

Pancake ice is a type of so-called pack ice. Ice freezes at the surface of the Polar Oceans and swims on top of the water. But the ice crust is continually broken up by rough sea. Little plates of ice are created with raised rim edges where they have collided with other plates. The plates take on the shape of pancakes.

You know what an ice-cream wafer is, but what is pancake ice?

A large part of the Arctic Ocean is covered with pack ice all year round. Especially in winter, the seas can only be navigated with special ships called icebreakers.

What are icebreakers used for?

Icebergs consist of freshwater.

Pack ice covers all the Arctic seas in winter. They can then only be navigated by icebreakers.

What is the colour of water?

Water is transparent. But in the sea and in rivers it appears to be blue from a certain depth. There are also rivers with black and white water. Rivers with white water flow through areas with a soft ground. The rivers carry off light-coloured clay that gives the water its white appearance. The Amazon is a white-water river. But another river of the Amazon Basin, the Rio Negro, flows through bog forests and is a black-water river. Black earth gives it its colour.

Is freshwater sweet?

Freshwater does not have to be sweet. By and large, the taste is completely neutral. However, some freshwater can taste decidedly sour or bitter, according to the minerals dissolved in it. But most water is to be found as saltwater in the oceans: 97.6 per cent of the world's water reserves.

Why are dams built?

To produce electricity from water. A hydro-electric power station channels the water through turbines inside the dam. Mountainous countries with a lot of rainfall, such as Norway, cover a large part of their energy needs this way.

The Iguaçu waterfalls lie on the border between Argentina and Brazil. Water plummets into the depths over the 2,700-metre (8850-foot) width of the waterfalls.

Many big rivers begin as small mountain streams.

There are both white-water and black-water rivers in the Amazon Basin.

Many rivers have their beginnings in the mountains. Melt water and rain join together in fast-flowing, clear, steep streams. Many mountain streams flow together in the valley to form a wide river. The river created by various tributaries then flows in a snake-like course over the flatter terrain. The nearer it gets to the sea, the wider and richer in water it becomes.

How does a river change on its way to the sea?

The Upper Rhine used to snake its way sluggishly through the landscape. It could scarcely be used by shipping. At every high water it sought a new course and flooded wide stretches of land along it banks. The river's course was straightened in 1817 and shortened by 80 kilometres (50 miles). In those days, no one knew about the disadvantages that river regulation brings with it. The river became faster because it didn't have to flow around so many curves, started to cut its way into the landscape and lowered the level of groundwater, the water from which the plants on the fields live. And when a large amount of rain falls in the mountains it is no longer slowed down by the river's course. Flooding is therefore more severe than before river regulation.

Why is the Rhine 80 kilometres shorter now than it used to be?

Estuary is the name given to a wide, funnel-like opening at the mouth of a river, where it flows into the sea. Here plant and animal species that are usually found only on land, or in rivers, or in the sea can be found mixed together.

What is an estuary?

Waterfalls are created on the upper reaches of rivers. They are formed where a river crosses a layer of hard rock bordering a softer layer. The softer layer is washed away more quickly. A terrace is formed. Niagara Falls plummets over a 50-metre (165-foot) high dolomite bank on leaving Lake Erie.

How are water-falls created?

What is a watershed?

A watershed is usually a mountain that determines in which direction a river flows. The line that determines in which sea a river flows is known as a continental watershed. The European Watershed runs through Germany: the Rhine, Oder and Elbe flow to the North Sea and Baltic Ocean. The Danube flows to the Black Sea to the southeast.

Why is it dangerous to bathe in a river?

Eddies can still occur even when a river is flowing at a leisurely pace. They are created by potholes in the river bed. The water spirals upward and is a danger to bathers.

Why are navigable rivers always being dredged?

Rivers are continually deepening their beds. In doing so they free rocks and soil and transport them downriver. The nearer a river approaches the sea, the smaller its cargo has become. The rocks give way to sand, and finally to floating particles. Where a river flows slowly, the stones and sand it has carried along are deposited. They make the river shallower but wider. Channels have to be kept clear to prevent ships form running aground.

The rocky shallows near the Loreley rock were feared by sailors on the Rhine.

What does the Loreley do?

The Loreley is a 132-metre (433–foot) cliff on the Rhine in Rhineland Palatinate, Germany. The shallows and rocks of the narrow section of the river are difficult to judge and a danger for shipping. Poems tell of a beautiful girl supposed to sit on the rock and lure sailors to their fate. But that is only the stuff of legends!

Which is Germany's longest river?

The Danube is the longest river flowing through Germany. However, on its 2,890-kilometre (1,800-mile) journey it also travels through nine other countries: Austria, Slovakia, Hungary, Croatia, Serbia, Rumania, Bulgaria, Moldavia and the Ukraine.

The Danube flows through ten different countries, here through the Hungarian capital Budapest.

Rivers are divided into categories according to their flow conditions. Periodic rivers exist only at specific times of year, for example during the thaw in spring. Episodic rivers, on the other hand, are often torrential but last for only a few days. They occur after heavy rainfall in the desert. Perennial rivers like most European rivers flow along their riverbeds throughout the year.

Delta is a Greek letter that looks like a triangle. Wide river mouths are also called by this name because they have a similar shape. A delta forms when a river carries a lot of mud and sand with it. Sand and particles floating in the water are deposited where the freshwater of the river comes into contact with the salty water of the sea. The Danube and the Nile have particularly large deltas.

Which word is used for the mouth of a river – alpha, gamma or delta?

In early times, people or horses used to pull ships upstream with ropes. This job was called boat-hauling. Boats were usually carried downstream by the river current or the wind. The boat-haulers of the Volga were especially renowned. Haulers carried out very strenuous work, but were soon no longer required when steam boats made their appearance in the 19th century.

Who were the boat-haulers?

Bascule bridges are found on rivers navigated by ships. The bridge is simply opened up when a ship comes by that is too tall to pass under the bridge. The bridge is then closed again once the ship has passed.

What is a bascule bridge?

The water of the Nile is very important for Egyptian agriculture.

Many farmers look forward to high water. Especially in the world's more arid regions, periodic high water ensures that fields along the riverbanks are flooded. Rivers such as the Nile carry enough water to flood their banks only for a few months of the year. The soil of adjacent fields is then well watered. The farmers sow their crops when the water again retreats. The Nile floods were so important for the ancient Egyptians that their annual calendars were oriented around them. Today, a reservoir dam, the Aswan Dam, prevents the floods. The fields are now often barren.

Who is pleased by high water?

How is a lake created?

Lakes are amounts of water that have collected in inland depressions. These hollows or basins can develop in various ways. Sometimes individual stretches of water are cut off from the sea by the movements of the Earth. That is how the Caspian Sea was created. Some lakes form in volcanic craters or in valleys blocked by a volcanic eruption. Lake Toba on Sumatra is the world's largest crater lake. Erosion or eolic lakes form when wind or ice wears away the top layer of the ground.

What is a backwater?

Pools and ponds created on cut-off sections of a streambed are called backwaters. The water in them is just as old as all the other water on Earth – around three billion years old. Backwaters are formed when a stream seeks a new course and water is left behind in its old bed. Rivers also often leave large backwaters called bayous.

Are there wandering lakes?

Lop Nur in the Taklimakan Desert in China is called a wandering lake. In dry periods it loses a big proportion of its water. It fills up rapidly again during the rainy season, albeit seldom at exactly the same location.

Salt lakes have formed in the Californian deserts of the USA.

A crater lake was created on the Poas volcano in Costa Rico.

The Aral Sea in Central Asia is drying out more and more.

A natural body of standing water that does not dry out is called a pond. Ponds are so shallow that sunlight can penetrate right to the bottom. That is why many various types of water plants flourish here. Artificial ponds are also laid out, mostly for fish farming. A body of standing water so deep that no growth is possible on its bed is called a lake.

What is the difference between a pond and a lake?

No ships sail anymore on the Aral Sea between Kazakhstan and Uzbekistan. They are all laid up inland where there was once water. The water of the Syrdarya and Amudarya rivers that once flowed into the sea is today used for watering cotton fields.

Where are the fishing boats of the Aral Sea?

Many lakes in arid regions have no outlet. They are called terminal lakes. River water also contains salts. Only these salts remain when the water evaporates.

How are salt lakes formed?

The Caspian Sea is the world's largest lake, with a surface area of 393,898 square kilometres (152,000 square miles). The deepest is Lake Baikal in Russia, 1,637 metres (5,370 feet) deep.

Which is the world's largest lake?

COUNTRIES

There are 193 countries in the world. The people in these countries belong to a great number of different cultures and speak many different languages. Some wear very different clothes from us and eat things that are to us either unknown or very unusual. People in foreign countries often have different political opinions or other religious beliefs. They play different music and create exotic works of art. All these differences have already led to conflicts in the past and even wars. But they also give people the chance to learn from one another.

Why is it so warm in Africa?	The Equator runs through the middle of Africa. Here the sun shines down vertically onto the Earth. The land is warmed a great deal more by the sun's heat. High temperatures dominate all year round. A fifth of the continent is covered by rainforest, 40 per cent by deserts and 40 per cent by savannas.
Is there also snow in Africa?	Mount Kilimanjaro is Africa's highest mountain. It is an extinct volcano in Tanzania, not far from the Equator. Its peak does not melt because it is 5,895 metres (19,340 feet) high. It is always covered by snow. Even the snow-capped peaks of the Ruwenzori Mountains are over 5,000 metres (16,400 feet) high.
Are humans descended from apes?	Although we are similar to apes, they are not our grandparents. They could rather be termed our uncles and aunts. Humans and apes share the same ancestors. And these lived in Africa. Here the first humans evolved. Remains of human-like creatures that lived four million years ago have been discovered in Africa. The first "real" people, who already made stone tools, appeared two million years ago. Humans then spread to the other continents about one million years ago.

Chimpanzees and humans share the same ancestors. Both originate from Africa.

It is possible to get to know the country and its people, as well as sometimes observing rare animals, during a safari in Africa.

Even though there is a lot of misery on the African continent, the music there is often loud and full of the joys of life. There is a lot of singing, dancing, drumming and playing of music in Africa. Rhythmic music can be heard at all festivities. Black Africans were taken to America as slaves over a period of more than three hundred years. They continued to play their music in the new, strange land. What we call jazz, reggae, rock and pop music originated from it. This music then came to Europe from America. Many people couldn't stand it at first, and disparagingly called it "negro music". But we would not play Viennese waltzes or dance round dances today were it not for Africa. For what band can do without percussion instruments and drums?

Where are the roots of pop music?

The source of the 6,700-kilometre-long (4,163 miles) Nile lies in Uganda. It flows north through desert regions and finally enters the Mediterranean in Egypt. The Nile supplies people with water and is an important traffic route.

Which is the world's longest river?

On average, a mother in Burundi and Kenya gives birth to more than six children. Every second person in Africa is under the age of 20. But the children often have little time to play together. They have to work at an early age and cannot therefore go to school. People in Africa have as many children as possible in the hope that they will look after them in their old age. But child mortality rates are high, which means many children die while still small. That's also why parents want to have many children, so that at least some of them grow up.

How large are African families?

With a surface area of nine million square kilometres (3.5 million square miles), the Sahara is the largest desert in world. The Namib Desert and the Kalahari lie to the south of the Equator.

What are the names of Africa's hot deserts?

What can rock drawings tell us about Africa's history?

Africa's earliest rock drawings can be found in southern Namibia. They are between 25,000 and 27,000 years old. The themes of the pictures are completely out of place in the modern age. The mountainous area called Hoggar and Tassili n'Ajjer lies in the middle of the Sahara in southern Algeria. Thousands of rock drawings have also been found there. Most of them are about 5,000 years old. The people of the time drew pictures of wild animals: buffalo, giraffes, elephants, rhinoceroses, hippopotamuses and antelopes, none of which can still be found in the Sahara today. So the climate must have been more moist 5,000 years ago.

Prehistoric rock drawings show that Africa was once subject to a different climate.

How does desert sand from Africa reach us?

Sometimes we too get a hint of Africa. The hot, dusty mass of air that blows northward from the Sahara is called the sirocco. The sirocco appears in the Sahara as a warm and arid dust or sand storm. The air picks up moisture on its way over the Mediterranean and then becomes humid over Italy and Spain. Sometimes the sirocco reaches over the Alps and deposits its dusty cargo there. When the snow of the Alps is covered by red dust from Africa it is known as blood snow.

Sometimes the sirocco blows over the Alps and brings sand from the Sahara to Europe.

Nomads in Niger roam from place to place with their herds of cattle in search of grazing land.

How do nomads live?

People who have no settled home but roam across the land with their animals are called nomads. They live in tents throughout the year. The nomads of the Sahara and East Africa roam with herds of camels, sheep and goats.

What does Mosi-oa-Tunya mean in English?

Mosi-oa-Tunya means "Smoke that Thunders" and is the name for the Victoria Falls in Africa. These waterfalls are 108 metres (350 feet) high and 1.5 kilometres (1 mile) wide. Small droplets of water form as the water plummets into the depths, rise into the air and look like smoke.

The San people, called Bushmen in the past, have adapted well to the dry climate of the Kalahari. Roots show them where groundwater is near the surface. They live as hunters. They also feed on roots and berries.

How can people survive in the Kalahari?

From the 16th century onward, the European countries of France, Great Britain, Portugal, Belgium and later Germany divided up Africa amongst themselves. As colonial rulers they wanted to profit from Africa's resources.

What are colonial powers?

The present state borders were drawn up in colonial times without regard to the tribal areas of the inhabitants. Although African countries are today independent, old tribal conflicts often resurface.

Why are there so many civil wars in Africa?

Which languages are spoken in Canada?

Most children in the province of Quebec speak French as their first language. Canada originally belonged to France because the French were the first European immigrants. But England later conquered Canada. Today, everyone in Canada has to learn English. French-speaking children not only have lessons to learn English, they are also taught some subjects in the foreign language.

What's the connection between Canada and the canoe?

Canoes were the fishing boats of the Inuit, then indigenous people of Canada's Arctic region. A canoe has no rudder. It is steered with a spade paddle. The canoeist kneels in the boat and pushes the paddle through the water on the side of the canoe. Canoes are still used today in rowing.

How were ice craters created?

Have you ever put a bottle of water in the freezer and forgotten about it? The bottle bursts because ice needs more space than water. Something similar happened with the ground in Canada. But it couldn't burst when underground water froze, so bulges formed instead. Theses bulging hills are called ice craters or pingos.

Only 32 million people live in Canada. Large parts of the country are uninhabited.

Canoes are boats. They are also used in white-water sport competitions.

The Inuit once attributed magic powers to the game of skill called Ajaqaq. It is played in early spring because it is supposed to hasten the return of the eagerly awaited sun. A walrus tusk is held in the hand as a handle. A rabbit's head is attached to it with a sinew. The player has to try to impale the head on the tusk.

How do you play Ajaqaq?

Only around 32 million people live in Canada. Canada is so big that on average it has only 2.3 people for every square kilometre!

How many people live in Canada?

Yes. Maple trees are tapped in spring in Canada. The sap drips into tin buckets on the trees through taps bored into the bark. The sap is boiled in vats until only a sweet caramel-tasting syrup remains. 40 litres of sap is needed for one litre of syrup.

Does maple syrup drip from the trees in Canada?

The Canadian flag is red and white with a red maple leaf in the middle.

What does Canada's flag look like?

The maple leaf can even be seen on Canada's flag.

Who is a citizen of the USA?

Anyone born in the USA is an American citizen. Even if a plane flying from Canada to Panama landed in the USA to refuel and a woman onboard gave birth, that child would be a citizen of the USA.

Do all children in the USA go to school?

Some children have such a long way to travel to school that their parents prefer to teach them at home. Children in Alaska usually learn to read and write at home. There are also children in the major cities that do not go to school. Some families are very religious and are afraid that their children will learn things in school that contradict their religious beliefs. In the past, many people emigrated to America because their religion was not accepted in their homeland.

What are the indigenous peoples of America called?

The people already living north of Mexico before the arrival of the Europeans, and their descendents, were called Red Indians. This name is due to a mistake on the part of European seafarers. They believed they had landed in East Asia, called India in those days. Today Red Indians are known as "Native Americans".

Brown bears also live in the USA's National Parks.

By no means are all parts of the USA as densely populated as Los Angeles.

American football is one of the most popular sports in the USA. There are also many school teams.

No, they spend almost the whole day in school, eat there and play a lot of sport in the afternoons. Every school has its school teams and the whole school cheers them on when they play in competitions.

Many people in the USA move often, because they have found work in another state. They then sell their homes and buy new ones nearer their place of work. But some people find it a nuisance always trying to find a new place to live. They live in mobile homes. These are houses on wheels that are hung on a lorry, allowing people to move with ease!

What are mobile homes?

The 13 British colonies in North America declared their independence from the mother country on 4 July 1776. They formed a state of their own. This day has been the national Holiday of the USA, Independence Day, ever since.

When do Americans celebrate their national Holiday?

North America is more than twice as large as Europe. But almost half the continent is scarcely inhabited. The north is covered with thick forests or lies under ice and snow. This is where the Inuit and Native Americans live. Other parts of North America are mountainous or arid and infertile. Only a few people live in these regions. Temperatures of up to 57 °C have been recorded in Death Valley in California. The major cities of North America are Los Angeles and New York in the USA. Many National Parks have been set up in North America to protect nature. The highest waterfall in North America can be found in Yosemite National Park. Moose and bears live in Yellowstone and Grand Teton National Parks. Alligators feel at home in the swampy regions of the southeast USA.

Is all of North America densely populated?

Which land-scapes can be found in South America?

The world's largest tropical rainforest lies in South America: the Amazon Basin. Giant rainforest trees also grow in Guyana and Venezuela. A high range of mountains can be found to the west of the rainforests: the Andes. Large prairies spread out to the south: the pampas of Argentina and Patagonia. There are desert regions further west. The Atacama Desert in northern Chile is the driest region of South America.

Where do many of our cut flowers come from?

There are enormous greenhouses in Colombia. A large proportion of the cut flowers sold in flower shops around the world are grown in them. The greenhouses are located alongside the airport because cut flowers do not keep for long. The flowers are cut and then immediately flown away.

Where do Darwin's finches live?

Darwin's finches, giant tortoises, marine iguanas, and Galapagos cormorants all live on the Galapagos Islands that belong to Ecuador. The islands are a popular tourist destination. But only 40,000 visitors a year are allowed to set foot on them, in order not to disturb the islands' unique fauna. Darwin's finches are named after the biologist Charles Darwin. He studied the development of new species and how animals adapt to their living conditions. Finches were the first species of bird to settle on the Galapagos. Many different species developed from them, each with a different beak.

Who are the Olmec?

The Olmec were the original inhabitants of Central America. Their culture originated in the Mexican Highlands and stretched back as far 1,500 years BC. The Olmec carved gigantic stone figures. They are famous for their so-called colossal heads and stone altars. They also made little jade figures, very often depicting a jaguar.

Marine iguanas live on the Galapagos Islands.

Cut flowers from Colombia are sold all over the world.

Around 500 years ago a treaty was signed that divided up South America between Spain and Portugal. Portugal received the eastern part that is now Brazil. The western part went to Spain. That is why today Portuguese is spoken in Brazil and Spanish in almost every other South American country. The Indian languages still widely spoken are Quechua, Guarani and Aymara.

In Brazil – here the famous Copacabana Beach in Rio de Janeiro – people mainly speak Portuguese.

Four species of camelid live high up in the Andes at an altitude of 3,000 metres (9,800 feet) above sea level. All possess the characteristic of spitting when in a fight. Two species live wild, the guanaco and the vicuña. The vicuña supplies the finest and warmest wool that there is. The Indians herd the animals together once a year to shear them. Each animal delivers 300 grams of wool. Two further species live as domesticated animals, the lama and the alpaca. Both carry burdens and are a source of wool and meat.

What are vicuñas?

People in South America love music. Pan pipes are made from bamboo stalks. They sound muffled and somewhat wistful. Pan pipes are accompanied by the charango, a small guitar made from an armadillo shell.

What are South America's traditional musical instruments called?

Panama hats are actually made in Ecuador, and are only called Panama hats because they are shipped from harbours in Panama. The finely woven hats don't lose their shape even when stuffed in a suitcase. The best hats can even be pulled through a wedding ring! It can take a family up to three months to make such a hat from palm fibres.

Are Panama hats made in Panama?

Carnival in Rio de Janeiro is the world's most colourful festival. Groups of musicians and dancers parade through the city. The samba music that accompanies them came originally from black slaves. Many of the people in splendid costumes who take part in the carnival parades live in the poor settlements on the edge of the city, the favelas. They spend all year making their costumes, building floats and practicing their dances. And as soon as carnival is over, they begin preparing for next year's.

Where does the world's most colourful festival take place every year?

Where is the world's biggest livestock market held?

The wide grassy steppes known as the pampas can be found in Argentina. Large numbers of cattle graze there. The world's largest livestock market is held in the capital, Buenos Aires. 50,000 animals are sold by auction there every week.

What is a gaucho?

In Argentina, Uruguay and southern Brazil, the equivalent of the North American cowboy is called a gaucho. They tend to cattle and horses on the grassy steppes of the pampas. Many Native Americans also work as gauchos.

Where are the banana republics?

Many of our luxury goods come from Central America: bananas often come from Guatemala, Honduras and Belize. Cigars are imported from Cuba. Cocoa also comes from Central America. The cocoa plant grows mainly on large plantations. The workers who harvest them receive only a fraction of the price we pay for chocolate. Chocolate from fair-trade shops is more expensive so that the workers can receive enough money to live.

A large amount of coffee comes from Brazil.

The Spanish names of Central American cities such as Cordoba in Mexico, Granada in Nicaragua or La Palma in Panama tell us the country of origin of their founders. Central America was ruled by various European countries. They suppressed the native populations and turned the countries of the Caribbean into colonies. The Spanish gave many of the cities they founded names from their homeland.

Why have many Central American cities Spanish names?

Brazil cultivates around four million tons of coffee a year, and is thereby the world's biggest producer of coffee.

Where does most coffee come from?

Cuba is often called the Sugar Island because sugar accounts for half the country's exports. Sugar is made from sugar cane, a grass that grows up to seven metres (23 feet) in height. The mature canes are cut down with knives known as machetes. They are then pressed to extract their sweet juice.

Do you know where sugar grows?

Lake Titicaca lies in Peru and Bolivia at an altitude of 3,800 metres (12,500 feet). The lake is therefore the world's highest navigable body of water.

Where is Lake Titicaca situated?

The pyramids of Chichén Itzá in Mexico: the Maya and Toltec civilizations existed before the arrival of the Europeans.

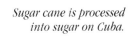

Sugar cane is processed into sugar on Cuba.

Which is bigger: Asia or the USA?

Asia is the world's largest continent. Much more than half the world's population are Asians, and one person in five is Chinese. But on television we hear far more about the USA than about the countries of Asia. When same-scale maps of Russia and the USA are placed alongside each other, it can be seen that Russia is almost twice as big. Asia is made up of 48 countries, of which both Russia and Turkey border on Europe.

Is Asia a rich continent?

The living standards in Asian countries vary greatly. Japan, Singapore and the states of the Persian Gulf are rich. But life is hard in Laos, Bangladesh or Kyrgyzstan.

One in five of the world's population lives in China. Here a street in Hong Kong.

Why do the Taiwanese brew tea several times?

When the Taiwanese brew their tea several times it is not a sign of thrift or stinginess. Indeed, the first brew from the tiny teapot is actually thrown away. It is bitter. The Taiwanese particularly like to drink green tea. The tealeaves are rolled by hand before drying. 100 grams of a precious tea can cost up to 500 Euros.

Monks at prayer: the Buddhist religion has its roots in Asia.

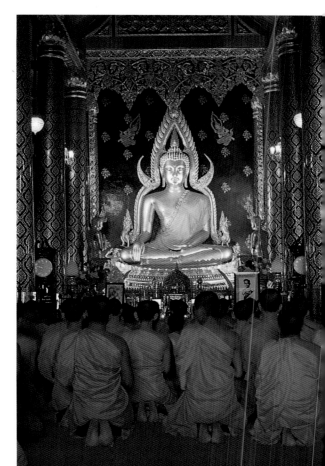

Asia exports many spices all around the world.

Which products originally came from Asia?

Many things that we today take for granted originally came from Asia: rice, tea, apricots, silk and many spices. In earlier times such goods were brought to us over the Silk Road by caravans.

Is the environment still intact in Asia?

Asia is a continent with enormous environmental problems: the rainforests are being destroyed. Rivers have been diverted in Central Asia to irrigate the deserts. That has changed the climate. Nuclear tests have contaminated large areas in Kazakhstan. And crude oil flows in the swamps in Russia from leaking pipelines.

Islam's roots are in Arabia, for its founder, Muhammad, was born in present-day Saudi Arabia. Jesus, the founder of the Christian religion, lived in Israel. Hinduism, Buddhism and Shinto are all Asian religions that also have many adherents in Europe.

As in Hollywood in the USA, many films are also made in the Indian city of Bombay. That's why the city is sometimes also called Bollywood.

Stretching for 6,350 kilometres (3,950 miles), the Great Wall of China is the world's biggest construction. It was built from the third century onward to protect China's northern border from the peoples of the steppes, is between three and nine metres high (10 to 30 feet) and can be seen with the naked eye from the international space station, ISS.

Which religions come from Asia?

What is Bollywood?

How long is the Great Wall of China?

How many islands make up Japan?

Japan consists of four main islands: Honshu, where the capital Tokyo is situated, Hokkaido, Shikoku and Kyushu. Another 3,000 islands also belong to Japan.

Why are the mountains of Asia so dizzyingly high?

The world's highest range of mountains, the Himalayas, lies in Asia. Mount Everest, at 8,848 metres (29,030 feet) the world's highest mountain, can be found there on the border between China and Nepal. But the other peaks of the Hindu Kush, Karakorum, Himalayas and Tien Shan are also dizzyingly high. That is meant literally, because air bubbles that damage the brain form in the blood at this height. People have headaches and feel dizzy, and can even die from altitude sickness.

Why do the Chinese chop their food?

In Chinese cuisine, the ingredients are chopped up into small pieces before they are cooked. Meat, fish, mushrooms and vegetables are not prepared whole because fuel in China has always been scarce and expensive. Meat cooks more quickly when cut up small. That saves energy. In addition, the vegetables retain many of their vitamins.

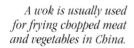

A wok is usually used for frying chopped meat and vegetables in China.

One part of the Turkish city of Istanbul lies in Europe, the other part in Asia. The city is divided into two parts by a body of water, the Bosporus Straits. It is possible to catch a ferry from Europe to Asia every ten minutes.

Which city straddles two continents?

Panda bears live in the mountain forests of South-west China. They eat about 600 bamboo canes a day. It takes them 16 hours to do so. A panda weighs only as much as a tangerine at birth. It rides piggyback on its mother and only starts to make steps of its own after three months.

How much does a panda bear eat?

Jackals live on the steppes in Armenia and in Iran. They look like small dogs, but are active at night. They communicate with other far-away jackals by howling. So jackals are not sad at all!

Are jackals sad when they howl?

The Hong Kong region of China is the world's most densely populated place. On average, 6,000 people live on one square kilometre of land. Hong Kong is an important centre of banking and commerce.

Where is the world's most densely populated area?

The Turkish city of Istanbul straddles two continents: Asia and Europe. The Hagia Sophia stands on the European side of the Bosporus.

At 8,848 metres (29,030 feet), Mount Everest is the world's highest mountain.

Where did native Australians come from?

The first settlers came to New Guinea and Australia simultaneously, around 50,000 years ago. They didn't even get wet doing so, because at that time the sea level was lower, and New Guinea was joined to Australia by a bridge of land. The descendents of these first settlers are called Aborigines.

How did rabbits get to Australia?

In 1859, Thomas Austin brought twelve rabbits to Australia to keep his lawn short. These rabbits had no natural enemies in Australia and therefore rapidly multiplied. Although people hunted them, there were around one billion rabbits in Australia by 1950, just over 90 years later. They became a plague on the country because they drove out native Australian animal species.

What is the Uluru?

The Uluru or Ayers Rock is a sandstone monolith in the Australian desert. It is about 3.6 kilometres (2.2 miles) long and 2 kilometres (1.2 miles) wide. The name Uluru comes from the language of the Aborigines. For them, the rock is a sacred site.

Kangaroos are the most well-known species of marsupial. They live in Australia.

There are many more sheep than people in New Zealand.

Ayers Rock or Uluru is a sacred mountain to the Aborigines.

Australia's large sheep farms are very far away from each other. The journey to school would be much too long for the children. Instead they are taught at home by radio and television. They talk to their teachers by radio transmitter. Their homework books are passed on to planes that bring them into the city.

How do sheep farmers' children talk to their teachers?

A kiwi fruit is a hairy brownish fruit with light-green flesh that tastes slightly sour. Extensive kiwi plantations can be found in New Zealand. The kiwi is also a bird species in New Zealand. It has a very long thin beak and cannot fly.

What are kiwis?

3.5 million people and 52 million sheep live on the two islands that make up New Zealand. The sheep are guarded by sheepdogs. Some sheepdogs manage to herd and round up the sheep without barking. They merely have to give the sheep a stern look. Regular sheep-shearing competitions are held in New Zealand. A top shearer can manage up to 350 animals a day. Shearing doesn't hurt the sheep. The wool grows back the same way our hair does.

Are there more people in New Zealand than sheep?

Marsupials evolved in Australia. Especially well-known are the koala bear, the opossum and the kangaroo. Marsupial babies are born at a very early stage of development. In contrast to other mammals, they cannot suckle on their own. They are also still blind at birth. But baby kangaroos and koalas still find their way through their mother's fur to her pouch, in which they find her teats. They cling tightly to them and the milk is injected into them by their mother. A kangaroo baby stays up to eight months in its mother's pouch.

Why do kangaroos have pouches?

Where is the international dateline?

When you call New York at noon, the person you're calling is eating breakfast. The further east you are, the later it is. Ultimately there's a border beyond which it is no longer today but tomorrow: the date is advanced by a day. This dateline runs through the middle of Oceania, between Tonga and Samoa.

Where in the Pacific do the densest forests grow?

New Guinea is densely forested. It rains a lot there. Countless streams and rivers have their sources in the mountains in the island's interior. They flow through areas of grassland and swamps on the coast. But the soil on most pacific islands is not deep enough for trees.

Where could you once pay with stones?

Money was always heavy on the Micronesian island of Yap. In earlier times, people there paid for thing with stones, just as people in the west paid for things with gold. This stone money looked like a millstone and had a hole in the middle. A pole could be put through this hole so that two people could carry a "coin". Several of these stones have been kept in every village on Yap. Around 6,000 of them still exist today. The stones were so valuable because they couldn't be produced on the island. They were brought to Yap by ship, something that wasn't easy in the days before motorboats.

What is the Lapita culture?

Lapita is the name of a human civilization that existed in Polynesia as early as 1,500 BC. The origins of this culture probably lay in New Guinea. The people who lived from agriculture kept dogs and chickens. Many pottery items from the time, some very ornately decorated, have been found.

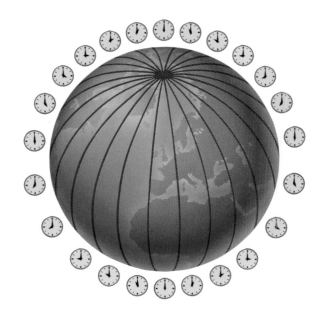

The Earth is divided into 24 time zones. The dateline runs through the middle of Oceania.

Wetness does not damage coconut fibres. That's why ropes and brushes can be made from them.

Around 25,000 islands are dotted over the South Pacific. But only a few thousand of them are inhabited. They were settled more than 10,000 years ago from Southeast Asia. Today, the Pacific Islands are divided into three large groups: Polynesia in the east, Melanesia in the south and Micronesia in the north. The people of the region live from fishing, mining and tourism.

Most islands in Oceania are small coral atolls.

How are tattoos done in Polynesia?

Tattooing is a typical Polynesian art form. The patterns are scratched into the skin with deep cuts. The ink is made by burning grubs. The wounds are also often filled with a rubbery mass made from cowry snails.

Who lived on Norfolk Island?

The crew of a ship called the "Bounty" mutinied in 1789 in the South Seas. The mutiny was crushed and the mutineers initially sent to the Pitcairn Islands, then settled on Norfolk Island. The island had already been used as a penal colony. In this way Australia was spared the cost of building prisons. Australia has repeatedly offered to include Norfolk Island in the Australian Commonwealth. But the inhabitants are not interested. They live from tourism. 30,000 tourists a year visit the island, which lies 1,400 kilometres (870 miles) to the east of Australia.

Where is material made from tree bark?

The paper mulberry tree grows on the Fiji Islands. Its bark is removed, soaked and beaten flat. Several layers are laid on top of each other and used to make clothes, blankets and jewellery.

What can be made from coconuts?

Coconut palms grow on all pacific islands. They can grow up to 30 metres (98 feet) high. People use the palm trees to make many products. Coconut fibres are very damp proof. That is why they are used to produce ships' ropes, coconut mats, carpets and brushes, or woven to make hammocks. The meat of the nut tastes very good. Coconut meat contains 37 per cent fat, which doesn't burn even at high temperatures. For this reason it is good to use for frying. Coconut milk is a delicious drink. The shells are ideal for serving food and drinks when cut in half.

Where is Europe at its hottest and where is it coldest?

In Northern Europe it is cold, while in the south it is very warm. Hardly anything grows in the far north where the ground is frozen for a long time in winter and spring. Elks live in the coniferous forests in Scandinavia. Here, people sweat mainly in the sauna. Mixed woods of deciduous and coniferous trees grow in Central Europe. In summer the sun's rays burn hot on the ground of Southern Europe. Here we find the fig cactus or the agave and plants with thick leathery leaves, the surfaces of which protect the stored water from evaporation.

Where is the world's tallest church spire?

With a height of 161 metres (528 feet), the tower of Ulm Minster is the world's tallest church spire. It took around 500 years to build it. The gigantic Gothic church can hold up to 20,000 people.

Is Mont Blanc Europe's highest mountain?

Mont Blanc is the highest mountain of the Alps. Its peak is 4,807 metres (15,771 feet) high. But that doesn't make it Europe's highest mountain. With a height of 5,642 metres (18,510 feet), Mount Elbrus in the Greater Caucasus is significantly higher – and it is growing by ten centimetres (four inches) every year.

The tower of Ulm Minster is the world's tallest church spire.

Agaves grow in Southern Europe.

Europe is not a continent surrounded by water – like Africa or Australia. Europe and Asia together form one continental plate. They are joined together at the Urals, a mountain range in Russia, and at the Caucasus, a range of mountains between the Black and Caspian Seas. And so there are countries that lie partly in Asia and partly in Europe: Russia and Turkey.

Where does Europe end?

No. On average, the sun shines ten hours a day in Stockholm in July, in January one hour. In Zurich in Switzerland it also shines for one hour a day in January. However, Zurich has on average only eight hours of sunshine a day in July.

Is it true that the sun shines less often in Stockholm than in Zurich?

Finland has beyond doubt the most lakes in Europe, but the largest freshwater lake, Lake Ladoga, lies in Russia.

Where is Europe's largest freshwater lake?

The leading animals of herds of Alpine cattle wear bells because the pastures on the mountain slopes often don't have fences. This way the farmer can easily find his herd. But dairy cows milk usually stay close to the villages.

Why do cattle in the Alps wear bells?

Cows in the Alps often wear bells around their necks.

Which rivers are Europe's longest?

Europe's longest river is the Volga. It flows for 3,531 kilometres (2,194 miles) through Russia before entering the Caspian Sea. The second longest river is the Danube. It rises in Germany and reaches the Black Sea in Romania.

What does a glutton eat?

The glutton, or wolverine, lives in Sweden's forests. The animal's name comes from a mistranslation of the Old Swedish word "Fjellfräs", meaning "fell (mountain) cat", which worked its way into German as "Vielfraß", or "devours much" in English. But its name aptly fits its pronounced appetite. It devours everything it can catch. Its prey includes ptarmigans, other species of martin, squirrels, foxes, deer and elk calves. The animal looks like a cross between a martin, a dog and a bear. It can grow up to a metre in length.

Built for the 1889 World Exhibition, the Eiffel Tower was origina intended to be dismantled again in 1909. But the inhabitants of Paris liked it so much that the decision was made to keep it.

What do amber and tinned fish have in common?

Amber can often be found on the Baltic Ocean shoreline. The yellow pieces are so light that they swim on the water. Amber is actually not a stone, but former tree resin. Sometimes insects or plants that got stuck in the resin when it was still gluey can be discovered in amber. The amber has preserved these insects and plants. Cut off from the air, they were not able to rot or be eaten away. This is also how fish can be preserved in tins without it beginning to stink.

Plants and insects are often preserved in amber.

Berlin – here the Brandenburg Gate – was divided into two halves from 1961 to 1989.

Where do the names of Spain's Mediterranean coasts come from?

The names describe the characteristics of these stretches of coast. From north to south, they are: Costa Brava – Wild Coast, Costa Dorada – Gold Coast, Costa del Azahar – Orange Blossom Coast, Costa Blanca – White Coast, and Costa del Sol – Sun Coast.

When did Great Britain first go full-steam ahead?

Industry developed early in Great Britain because the steam engine was invented here in 1784. There was also enough coal and water for the machines. With these engines it was possible to spin wool, weave cloth and pull trains.

What are prefabricated high-rise blocks?

Most city-dwellers in former East Block countries live in prefabricated high-rise apartment blocks that are quick and easy to build, and in which all the apartments look the same. On almost every balcony, especially in Russia, you can see jars in which tomatoes, gherkins and jam are preserved for winter.

How many people visit the Eiffel Tower in a year?

Every year, around six million people visit the Eiffel Tower, France's major landmark. The Eiffel Tower was built in 1889 and is 300 metres (984 feet) high.

What was the Berlin Wall?

For 28 years, a concrete wall divided Berlin into two halves, West Berlin and East Berlin. The people of Berlin stormed this wall when the border between the German Democratic Republic and Federal Republic of Germany was opened in 1989.

ECONOMY

From hunters and gatherers to stock breeders and farmers with their own machines: no creature other than the human has understood throughout the history of its development how to shape nature according to its will.

Flourishing wheat fields grow on once barren soil thanks to modern methods of irrigation, and even remote places enjoy supplies of electricity and energy as a matter of course. But it is often forgotten in the face of such successes that even today humans are still dependant on nature, which has made our great achievements possible in the first place.

On what does humanity's existence depend?

People gain everything they need for life from the Earth's available materials: they sustain themselves from water, animals and plants; obtain energy from water, coal or oil; and build houses, cars and computers from metal, stone and plastics made from crude oil.

Are resources and raw materials the same thing?

Resources are all the materials and things that are naturally available to us humans, things such as sunlight or wind. Raw materials on the other hand are only those resources that are actually physical materials, such as wood, metals or crude oil.

What are non-renewable resources?

Non-renewable resources are materials that we use, but are not present in an unlimited supply. This includes crude oil, natural gas, coal and many metals. While some of these materials are still available in large amounts, the supply of others, such as crude oil from which we produce electricity and petrol, will dry up in the foreseeable future.

What are renewable resources?

People can use an unlimited amount of renewable resources because, in the case of plants, they grow again or, like sunlight or the wind, are continually present.

People can harness the inexhaustible energy of the sun with the help of solar panels.

The agricultural plants and crops people cultivate are also among the Earth's renewable resources.

Fossil fuels are materials such as coal, natural gas or crude oil that were created millions of years ago from the remains of plants and animals and are now usually to be found beneath the Earth's surface. Although in a strict sense they should really be classed as renewable resources due to their origins, the creation of fossil fuels takes such a long time that they are not considered renewable resources. Fossil fuels are at present the most important source of energy and the raw material for making numerous kinds of synthetic materials.

What are fossil fuels?

First, a distinction must be made between brown coal and anthracite. In some places, carbon-rich anthracite often lies buried deep under the surface beneath hundreds of metres of rock and therefore can only be accessed through a laborious deep-mining process. Less carbon-rich and therefore less valuable brown coal, on the other hand, can usually be found in large deposits just beneath the surface and can be extracted through opencast mining.

How is coal mined?

Crude oil can be found under all continents and under the seabed. The most important deposits are in the Middle East, in Saudi Arabia and Iraq for example, but there are also rich deposits in Russia, Africa, Indonesia and even under the North Sea.

Where can crude oil be found?

Present estimates suggest that if global energy consumption remains constant, and unless significant new reserves are discovered, the existing oil reserves will be used up by around the year 2040. Many known deposits are so inaccessible that it is not worthwhile exploiting them.

How long will supplies of oil last?

How is petrol manufactured?

Petrol is made from crude oil. Crude oil is pumped from the depths of the Earth and then freed from troublesome components in refineries. The results are products of various qualities, ranging from heating oil, diesel and petrol to the materials for manufacturing plastics, detergents and medicines.

Can petrol also be made from vegetable oil?

Conventional petrol cannot be made from vegetable oil, but a form of diesel fuel can be made from rapeseed oil. Biodiesel can be used to fuel diesel vehicles.

What other sources of energy do we use?

Most of the energy we use today is produced from coal, crude oil and natural gas. Other major sources we make use of are nuclear energy obtained from uranium as well as wind and water power.

How can energy be produced from wind and water?

Present-day electricity is based on a generator that creates energy from a turning turbine. Wind or fast running water can also be used to provide the necessary rotation.

The significance of wind energy in meeting the world's demand for electricity is growing steadily.

Biodiesel can be made from vibrant yellow rapeseed plants.

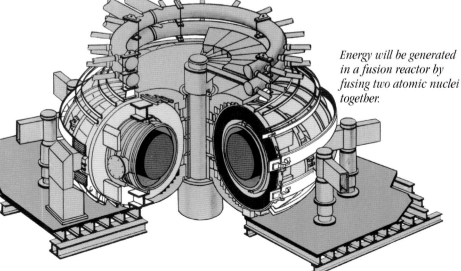

Whereas solar cells transform the sun's energy into electricity directly, solar heaters first heat water to provide a house with warmth or to generate electricity indirectly through turbines. This process is more complicated but it produces much more electricity.

How can solar energy be used?

There is indeed: the moon is responsible for the high and low tides of the oceans. This flow of large amounts of water back and forth generates a great deal of electricity in tidal power stations.

Is there such a thing as lunar energy?

The atomic fission of a nuclear power station generates enormous amounts of energy, but the resulting radioactive waste is very dangerous. Therefore some countries, for example Germany, want to gradually close down all their nuclear power station.

Does nuclear power have a future?

Many scientists hope they will one day be able to copy the nuclear fusion that takes place in the sun to create energy on Earth. Should they be successful, these fusion power stations could be the future's source of energy.

What is a fusion power station?

Energy will be generated in a fusion reactor by fusing two atomic nuclei together.

Where are metals found?

Metals such as iron, gold, copper or aluminium are found either pure or in combination with other materials in so-called ores. An ore is a mineral rock with a metal content so high that it is economically worth extracting.

What is the Earth's most common metal?

Aluminium is the Earth's most common metallic element although it is never found in a pure form. It is extracted from the aluminium ore bauxite and because of its light weight and great stability it is used for vehicle construction, the manufacture of household articles and in the electrical industry. The largest deposits of bauxite are found in Australia, which is estimated to account for more than 60 per cent of the world's reserves.

What was the goldrush?

When large finds of gold were discovered in some regions of North America and Australia in the 19th century, thousands of people poured into the areas to try their luck as gold diggers. Way over 80,000 people made their way to the American west coast in 1849 alone.

The electricity generated in a power station is transported to the sockets of our homes by means of kilometres of copper cables.

The roof of this temple is completely covered in gold. The splendour of the gods is expressed through such constructions.

Quartz sand provides the raw material for highly sensitive silicon plates without which no computer could be built.

Gold leaf really does consist of gold, but it is rolled out extremely thinly to decorate books or gild church interiors. Gold leaf is only a micrometre thick, that's one thousandth of a millimetre.

What is gold leaf made from?

All metals were created the same time as the Earth itself, that was about five billion years ago. But copper was the first metal to be used by man. The oldest finds of copper spearheads and small pieces of jewellery date back to between 8,000 and 9,000 years ago. The first traces of iron processing in the Middle East date back to 4,800 BC, whereas the Iron Age in Europe began as late as around 1,000 BC.

Which metal is the oldest?

Electricity and telephone cables are usually made of copper. It is a common and easy to process metal, a good conductor of electricity and often used in alloys.

What are electricity cables made of?

Minerals are chemical elements or compounds present in the Earth's crust. Minerals include metals such as copper, gold and silver, as well as gems like diamonds, emeralds, sapphires and opals.

What are minerals?

The body needs very small amounts of minerals to survive, but enough of these are provided by the food we eat and particularly the water we drink. Salt, a mineral we use in the kitchen, is a special case. Salt is not only dug out of salt mines, it is also largely obtained from the sea. For this, seawater is channelled to large flat areas near the shoreline where it can slowly evaporate, leaving only salt behind.

Are minerals edible?

How long have people been farming?

The first humans occupied themselves as hunters and gatherers. They ate only animals they had killed while hunting and the plants and berries they found growing around them. It was only around 9,000 years ago that man began to keep animals, thereby freeing himself from reliance on success as a hunter, and to cultivate cereal crops such as wheat and barley.

What do people eat?

The European diet is extremely diverse; however, the number of basic foodstuffs that give people sustenance here, as in the world's poorer countries, is not very large. The most important role is played by plant foods, including cereals. These include wheat and barley, but also maize, rice and millet, which mainly grow in the world's warmer regions. Globally, the main species of animals eaten are cattle, pigs, sheep and chickens.

Rice is one of the most important crops in the world's warmer regions.

Where does the potato come from?

Many people think we have always had potatoes, but that's not true. In the 16th century, seafarers brought the tubers from America to Spain, from where it quickly spread throughout Europe. Tubers play an important dietary role all over the world. Where potatoes don't grow very well, people eat cassava, sweet potatoes or yam roots.

Why do we need fruit and vegetables?

Whereas cereals and tubers are necessary to cover people's basic nutritional needs, fruit and vegetables supply additional substances that help us stay healthy. They contain many vitamins, minerals, roughage and so-called secondary plant compounds. Many poor people in developing countries eat only the basic nutritional foodstuffs and fall ill easier than people who live in Europe.

Tractors and other machines make the laborious task of farming much easier for many farmers.

The importance of agriculture is often forgotten by the population of the industrial nations who mostly live in towns and cities. It actually represents one of mankind's most significant achievements. Without the help of animal husbandry and agriculture – regardless of whether carried out by hand or with the help of colossal harvesting machines – nature alone would not be able to feed all the people who presently live on Earth.

Do all farmers have tractors?

Whereas almost every farmer in the industrial nations owns tractors and combine harvesters, or extensive stall equipment and milking machines, the people in poor countries have to make do with simpler aids such as axes, scythes and hand ploughs.

Where does milk come from?

Cattle provide the largest proportion of milk production. The milk is needed not just for drinking, but also for making many other dairy products such as cream, butter and cheese. But sheep, goats, camels and even horses are also used for milking.

Which meat do we eat most?

Although there are far more chicken, cattle, sheep and goats in the world than pigs, the consumption of pork is higher than that of all other sorts of meat. This is because most other species are not kept just for their meat, but also for their milk or eggs.

What do free range, deep litter and battery cage mean?

Chicken farming became ever more industrialised to try and meet the enormous demand for hen's eggs. This led to battery cages where thousands of hens were cramped together in cages to lay their eggs. The animal welfare movement protested against this and demanded eggs from hens kept under more ethical conditions appropriate to the species. Deep litter hens can run about indoors on the floor, free range hens can wander about in the open air.

Which is the commonest cereal?

Wheat tops the list of cereal production in Europe, Australia and North America. It is used to make flour, bread and pasta. In warmer regions rice grows better. It is eaten directly as a food, or also processed to make flour, oil and other products.

The pig is one of the few domesticated animals kept for its meat alone.

Are genetically manipulated foods dangerous?

There is no agreement on this question. No short-term harm has been proved, but at the moment most people do not want to buy genetically manipulated foods because they fear possible long-term effects and because environmentalists are afraid that such plants could eliminate the original species.

How important is soil quality?

Not every type of soil or ground is suitable for agriculture. Plants flourish best in deep, humus-rich soil with plenty of minerals, such as loessical soil, for instance.

What is fertilizer made from?

Fertilizers are material or compounds that are added to the soil to increase crop yields. In the past farmers used animal manure or composted vegetation, today they overwhelmingly use artificial fertilizers that contain nitrogen, phosphorus, potassium and sodium.

What is compost?

Composting is the decomposition of organic material by microorganisms, worms, woodlice and other small creatures. The final product is called compost. Finished compost is an excellent fertilizer and a very good soil conditioner.

Pests were repeatedly the cause of massive crop failures before the introduction of pesticides.

Heavy machinery is essential for sensible forestry management.

Crops failed repeatedly in the past due to drought or damage caused by pests. In the 19th century hundreds of thousands of Irish people starved because the entire potato harvest failed. Crop failures have become more seldom thanks to pesticides and fertilizers, but even today crops can fail in countries with a hot climate due to periods of drought.

What is a crop failure?

They are substances applied to plants to protect them from pests and diseases. They have contributed to making harvests more secure. However, these substances are also often harmful to people, so that they are only used in moderate amounts.

What are pesticides?

With only a few exceptions, all our forests are commercially managed and have been planted by man. Forest wardens and forestry workers are responsible for managing the forests. They fell trees for the paper and furniture industries and then plant more trees to replace them.

Do we still have primeval forests?

The daily newspaper is printed on paper made from the wood of forest trees.

When did the fishing industry begin?

People began to catch and eat fish or mussels and sea snails from the seas and lakes and rivers more than 100,000 years ago, during the Old Stone Age. The first boats were built around 8,000 BC, and some people specialised in catching fish.

Which kinds of fish are caught?

Fish are usually divided into freshwater fish and sea fish. Freshwater fish live in rivers and lakes: many types of trout, carps, pike or whitefish, for example. Tuna, herrings, cod, mackerels and plaice are among the sea fish.

The fishing boats of the North Sea are used to catch herrings as well as other fish.

What is seafood?

The term seafood covers all the sea animals we eat except for fish. This mainly includes mussels, oysters, crabs, shrimps, crayfish, lobsters and squid.

Are whales the largest fish?

The sea's largest inhabitant, the whale, is a mammal and not a fish. Most countries have agreed to stop hunting whales because their numbers have declined sharply. Japanese and Norwegian whalers nevertheless still hunt these giants of the sea.

Fishing nets are often fastened to several ships and then drawn through the water.

Fresh fish like this rainbow trout are laid on ice in shops.

What kinds of fishing are there?

There are three categories of fishing: deep sea fishing, coastal fishing and freshwater fishing, which is carried out on rivers and lakes.

What is aqua farming?

Just as people keep pigs, cattle and chickens on farms, they also breed some species of fish and other sea creatures such as mussels, oysters and squid. This is called aqua farming, from "aqua" (water) and farming. The biggest role in this is played by the breeding of trout, salmon, halibut and carp.

How are fish caught?

People who catch fish for their own needs or as a hobby use a fishing rod. Professional fishing is mainly done with nets, fishing lines or fish traps. The nets are either set up in a fixed place or drawn by boats. Fishing lines are used to catch tuna, for example. There are many types of fish traps.

Are all fish eaten?

Around a third of the fish caught is processed in factories to make fish meal for feeding animals.

What is a by-catch?

When fishermen use large nets and long fishing lines they don't always catch the sort of fish they're seeking. For example, the by-catch of dolphins while fishing for tuna is well known and much criticised. Almost a third of all creatures caught – that is around 30 million tons a year – are thrown back overboard unused, often either already dead or fatally injured.

ENVIRONMENT

Today, more than six billion people live on the Earth. They use an enormous amount of resources to keep themselves alive. This also places an enormous strain on the environment, people's natural surroundings. Households, industrial plants and vehicles pollute the air, water and soil are contaminated, and densely populated areas increasingly suffer from heightened levels of noise. But the biggest problem is global warming. National and international organisations, as well as political parties, are intensifying the fight against the destruction of the environment.

What is an ecosystem?

An ecosystem encompasses all the living things in a specific area and describes how they are dependent on the inanimate environment around them. For example, all the plants and animals that live in a lake, as well as the location of the lake, the state of the soil, the climate conditions and much more, are all part of a lake's ecosystem. On the other hand, the entire Earth can be seen as one self-contained ecosystem: energy is supplied by the sun and with its help vegetation creates substances that are utilised by other creatures.

Are ecosystems stable?

Ecosystems in densely populated regions like Europe are often disrupted. When people build roads or housing areas, straighten the course of streams and rivers, or use a lake for wind surfing in summer they interfere with the existing ecosystem, often with bad results for the animals and plants that live there.

What is a biotope?

A biotope is the space in which an ecosystem is settled. Not only natural surroundings such as forests, rivers or lakes can be regarded as biotopes. Artificially created places such as cities, railway tracks and even rubbish tips also offer animals and plants viable places to live.

The ecosystem of a lake, here one in Finland, includes all the animals and plants that live around it.

Plants produce the oxygen we need to survive.

Rainforests are the evergreen forests of the hot and humid tropics. Especially many species of animals and plants live in the rainforests. They also play an important role in the climate and environment of the entire world. The largest continuous area of rainforest lies in the Amazon region in South America.

How significant is the rainforest?

Oxygen is the commonest element on the surface of the Earth. It can be found both in the air and as a component of water, as well as in numerous rocks in the Earth's crust. The oxygen in the air is almost completely due to the ability of plants to give off oxygen during photosynthesis. All more developed creatures would suffocate if there were no plants!

Where does oxygen come from?

Species can die out for many different reasons, for groups of animals like the dinosaurs have always been disappearing from the face of the Earth. But humans have greatly increased the danger. Man has wiped out some species, like the bison, through hunting; others by changes to the ecosystem. And so only a few giant pandas still exist in China because the bamboo forests they eat have been chopped down.

Why do some species of animal become extinct?

A small part of the Earth's water reserves evaporates into the atmosphere where it forms clouds. The water falls as saltless rain either directly into the ocean or on land where it flows back into the sea through rivers or evaporates again beforehand.

How does the water cycle function?

Plants grow when they receive enough water and sunlight. They are eaten by herbivores who themselves fall prey to carnivores or omnivores. This system of dependency is called the food chain.

What is a food chain?

How many species of animal are there on Earth?

Around 1.1 million. Insects alone account for 750,000 of these. But there are only about 4,250 species of mammals – humans are one of them.

What happens when a species becomes extinct?

First of all, the numbers of animals continually decline until it becomes difficult for male and female animals to find one another. Sooner or later, the last of the species dies without having produced offspring.

Is it normal for species to die out?

Animals have always died out due to natural disasters or climatic changes such as the Ice Ages. But today, around 1,000 times more species are dying out due to man's interference with nature than in the past.

What can people do to prevent the extinction of species?

Nature protection reserves could be set up wherever possible. International agreements on banning hunting and fishing can help in other cases. Sometimes, endangered species can be saved from extinction by breeding them in zoos and later setting them free into the wild.

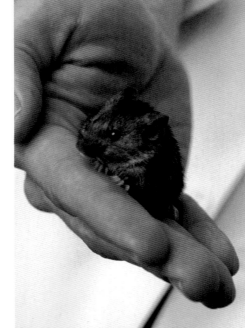

Newly developed medicines are often tested on animals.

It is especially in densely populated areas such as Europe that many species have already become extinct. The lynx, our region's only large wild cat, is today in danger of becoming extinct, for example. Only 15 of them can still be found in Germany.

Are species dying out in Europe?

Many species of butterfly and beetle are among the endangered insects. They suffer primarily from the ever-decreasing variety of plant life.

Are insects also endangered?

People have been keeping animals for their milk, meat or eggs for thousands of years. But animal farming has been industrialised over recent years and the living conditions have deteriorated greatly. Many conservationists therefore demand a ban on intensive animal farming.

How do people treat farm animals?

When companies develop new medicines or perfumes they have to test whether the new products are safe for people. Experiments are first of all carried out on animals because many of them react in a similar way to humans. However, the question is often asked whether people really should be allowed to mistreated and kill animals purely for cosmetic purposes.

Why do we need animal experiments?

In Europe the lynx is in danger of extinction.

A hen and a cockerel feel at home on top of a dung heap. But many farm animals are not so lucky and live their lives cramped closely together on factory farms.

When did environmental protection begin?

The tall chimneys of 19th century industrial factories could be considered the first attempt to protect the environment. The first nature protection reserves were set up in the 1920s. The modern concept of environmental protection began to be developed in the 1960s. The best-known agreement in international law is the Kyoto Protocol, adopted on 1 Dezember 1997.

What is smog?

In the past, smog was the foggy haze of soot and sulphur dioxide that factories and homes discharged mainly in winter. Today, this "winter smog" rarely occurs. "Summer smog" is the name given to heightened ozone levels measured over recent years in the air we breathe that occur by intensive sunshine.

What is the biggest threat to the environment?

Scientists believe that the increasing carbon dioxide levels in the air pose the greatest threat to the environment. This gas is released by burning fossil fuels and causes the so-called greenhouse effect. When carbon dioxide levels in the atmosphere rise, heat is prevented from escaping into space. Instead, carbon dioxide reflects it back to Earth, which warms up the climate.

The greenhouse effect can make our climate milder – or even cooler.

Motor car exhaust fumes damage the environment.

The nature protection reserve in the Luneburg Heath was set up early in the 20th century.

Both increased levels of carbon dioxide in the atmosphere and an increase in the global climate's temperature have been measured. The connection between global warming and carbon dioxide levels in the atmosphere is now beyond doubt.

Can the greenhouse effect be measured?

Glaciers and – more importantly – the ice at the poles are melting because it is getting increasingly warmer. This leads to a vicious circle, because ice cools the air and also reflects sunlight back into space. So when there is less ice the Earth becomes even warmer and more ice melts.

Why are glaciers melting?

No one knows for sure what the exact results of global warming will be. But plants that previously froze here in winter might well start growing well if average temperatures rise.

Will palm trees soon be growing in Central Europe?

The Earth's climate is a very complicated system, influenced by an infinite number of factors. European weather is determined by the Atlantic through the Gulf Stream transporting warm water northwards. The Gulf Stream could cease to flow if water melting from the poles changed the ocean temperature, then our climate would be a lot colder than now!

Why could global warming also lead to a new Ice Age?

For several years now, all cars with petrol engines must be fitted with a catalytic converter to reduce poisonous exhaust fumes. However, diesel motors operate without such a cleaning system and produce a lot of soot. Some manufacturers already offer soot filters to make these cars cleaner. But the best method of preventing exhaust fumes is to leave the car in the garage and travel by bike or train.

What can be done against exhaust fumes?

What is the ozone hole?

Scientists began to register a decline in the ozone levels of the upper layers of the atmosphere at the end of the 1960s, first over the Antarctic then later over the Arctic, too. There was so little ozone present, especially after the Polar winter, that people began talking of the ozone hole in the 1980s. Ozone in the atmosphere is very important because it protects us from the sun's ultraviolet rays.

What causes the ozone hole?

Scientists discovered that the major cause was a substance with which people were polluting the atmosphere: the chlorofluorocarbons, or CFC for short, used for example as a propellant for aerosols. Use of CFC was then banned almost completely.

Is the ozone hole growing?

Increases in the size of the ozone holes have been registered over the years, and it is only recently that the development appears to have come to a halt. Since it takes CFC 10 to 15 years to reach the ozone layer, it is hoped that this is the first success of the ban on CFC and that the ozone holes over the Poles will have closed again in 30 years' time.

How dangerous are ozone holes?

The sun's ultraviolet rays can cause damage to the skin and genes of living creatures. Protection against the sun's rays was significantly increased in Australia, which is close to the southern ozone hole. There, people were warned against spending time in the sun without protection.

How does summer smog counteract ozone holes?

It is true that the same substance that is so important for the atmosphere also causes summer smog in the air we breathe. But the ozone created near the ground does not find its way into the stratosphere but dissipates beforehand. Therefore summer smog is of no "help" in combating ozone holes.

People should not spend time in the sun in Sydney and many other places in Australia without protection.

People can become ill when they eat contaminated fish.

There are international groups championing the cause of the environment that do not seek to make a profit for themselves. One of the best known is Greenpeace, which was set up in 1971. Its members often go to places where disaster threatens or where one has already happened. They try to intervene through non-violent means. For example, oil tankers in danger are observed by activists in inflatable rubber boats. Greenpeace has around 2.83 million members.

What are the results of altering the course of rivers?

People have straightened the course of rivers in order to transport goods as quickly as possible by ship. This initially dried out many river flood plains that were home to rare plants and animals. These flood plains had also provided a natural way of cleansing a river, this was now missing. But most of all, the flood plains could soak up large amounts of water when a river was in full flood.

Have floods become more dangerous?

Flood water reaches towns on rivers much quicker and at a higher level than in the past because the water flows faster and the flood plains no longer exist.

Can the oceans also be polluted?

Due to the enormous amount of water in the oceans, no pollutant can poison all the seawater. But shipping and sewage discharge are concentrated around the coast, thereby heavily polluting the water.

What is oil pollution?

Oil pollution occurs when the seacoast is polluted by crude oil leaking from shipwrecked or damaged oil tankers. It usually results in the death of many seabirds and other animals. Oil pollution is fought by special ships that try to suck up the oil swimming on the surface.

Are people also threatened by pollution at sea?

When poisons find their way into the sea they are absorbed by all the creatures there. At the end of the food chain are fish, which not only absorb the poison directly but also indirectly by eating mussels and other microscopic creatures. This is why unhealthy substances such as heavy metals accumulate so much in fish. People themselves can then be harmed when they eat contaminated fish.

Many rare plants and animals live on river flood plains.

What is meant by population explosion?

The Earth's population was still only one billion people in 1804; at the time of Christ's birth it was only half that number. But since then the number of people has increased sharply, like an explosion. Today, more than six billion people live on the Earth, and the number is expected to rise to nine billion by 2054.

Will there be climatic disasters?

Scientists have been recording a steady increase in the warmth of the Earth's climate for about 100 years, and this increase has even quickened in recent years. The danger is that changes can happen so quickly that people do not have enough time to adjust. Very many people would be hit very hard if the coasts were suddenly flooded or fertile lands turned into deserts.

Can extinct animals be brought back again?

With advance in genetic technology, it could in future be possible to reconstruct extinct animals from preserved genetic material, the so-called DNA. But this requires intact DNA, which can survive in dead tissue for 10,000 years at most. So we'll never again see animals like the dinosaurs, which became extinct 50 million years ago.

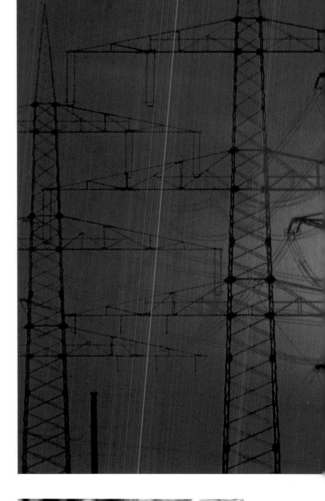

The world's population is exploding.

Environment protection has already achieved a lot in the world's rich countries, and in some respects the environment is more intact today than 30 years ago. Perhaps humanity will succeed in protecting and preserving nature to a great extent despite the dangers posed by the continually growing world population.

Will the destruction of the environment continue?

The crude oil used to make petrol and diesel fuels today will not last forever. Humanity has 40 to 50 years to find an alternative source of energy.

For how long will there be cars?

The universe is big beyond imagination. There might be other planets that offer good conditions for life. But using present technology a spacecraft would have to travel for thousands of years to reach them.

Are there other inhabitable planets?

The sun that sustains all life on Earth will continue to shine for roughly another five billion years and then go out. No living creature will survive this event. But who can tell if humans will still be around then?

For how long will life exist on Earth?

The sun will extinguish in roughly five billion years.

All accessible reserves of crude oil will be exhausted in this century. Alternative sources of energy must be found by then.

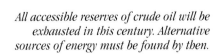

Picture credits: Archiv Naumann & Göbel (1) MEV (139), Miles Kelly Art Library (21), Photodisc (1), Picture Alliance (5), Uitgeverij Het Spectrum, B. V, (5); cover motif: Getty